THE PICTORIAL HISTORY OF
GOLF

BISON GROUP

Contents

Produced by
Bison Books Ltd.
17A Fulham Road
London SW3 6RL

Sir James Mac Donald
Natus 26 Se...

Alexander Mac Donald Esq...
Natus 2 March June 17...

Sir James Mac Donald
Natus 26 ...

INTRODUCTION

Because of its growth during the past hundred years and its present mass popularity, the history of golf in the 20th century is very easy to write about. It has certainly been well chronicled by historians and statisticians alike. But look back beyond the past hundred years and the history of this wonderful sport becomes more intriguing.

For a start, nobody can pinpoint the exact birth of golf. Many great golfing students and historians have tried in the past and have failed to come up with a definitive answer. Many good suggestions have been offered, and one cannot ignore them. We will look at the offered suggestions as to golf's beginnings but it will be up to you to decide which you prefer to choose as the right one.

Once we have 'established' golf's origins, the rest becomes easy as we look back at some of the people, events and courses which have contributed towards the growth and popularity of golf, starting with the pre-British Open days, and bringing you forward to the present day and such great players as Curtis Strange, Greg Norman and Severiano Ballesteros.

But will any of these modern golfers ever match the remarkable feats of the likes of Harry Vardon, who won the British Open a record six times; Bobby Jones who won the amateur and professional Opens of Britain and the United States . . . *in one year* Byron Nelson who won 11 successive US Tour events in 1945; and of course, will anybody ever equal the outstanding record of 18 major championship victories as a professional achieved by Jack Nicklaus?

Whether these outstanding achievements are equalled or bettered is irrelevant. Golf will remain a great game irrespective of whether records are broken or not. Golf will always provide records waiting to be broken, and golf will always provide personalities.

Ian Morrison

PAGE 1: *John Whyte Melville, painted by Francis Grant in 1874. Melville was twice elected Captain of the Royal and Ancient Club but died before his second term in office.*

PAGE 2-3, MAIN PICTURE: *The greatest golfer of all time? Jack Nicklaus on his way to his record-breaking win in the 1986* Masters. His caddy is his son, Jack jnr.

PAGE 2, INSET TOP: *Byron Nelson, whose achievements in the 1945 season are unlikely ever to be equalled.*

PAGE 2, CENTER: *Two of the finest players of the 1930s, Densmore Shute (driving) watched by his* opponent Henry Cotton.

PAGE 2, BOTTOM: *Greg Norman recovers from a bunker during the final round of the 1989 British Open.*

PAGE 4-5: *Jose Maria Olazabal during the 1989 Ryder Cup. Olazabal is many people's tip for the top for the 1990s.*

LEFT: *A charming study of a young Scottish enthusiast from the mid eighteenth century, 'The MacDonald Boys' by an unknown artist. Note the shape of the club.*

ABOVE: *A 'golfing' scene forms part of the decoration on an early sixteenth century Flemish Book of Hours.*

THE ORIGINS OF GOLF

Unlike many sports, golf does not enjoy the privilege of knowing its exact birthright. Several countries lay claim to being the 'home' of golf, notably England, France, Holland and Scotland. All such claims are *bona fide* and, despite many years of research by leading writers, historians and statisticians, there has been no tendency to favor one or the other.

If you think about it logically, golf, like so many other bat and ball games, could have been, and most probably was played in ancient times. In golf's case it would not have been with a high technology graphite-shafted club, and the very best of golf balls. Equipment would probably have consisted of a branch off a tree and a stone played to a target but this would have been golf in all but name.

Coming forward a few hundred years to the mid 14th century and to Gloucester Cathedral we find that a stained glass window was commissioned by a certain Sir Thomas Broadstone to commemorate comrades who fell at the Battle of Crecy. The window

clearly depicts a man swinging a club at a ball. Is this the first reference to golf? If so, where was the game played? All the window depicts is a man swinging a club at a ball. It could have been that Sir Thomas's colleagues played 'golf' while waiting to go into battle. Or was it depicting somebody playing the game of *cambuca* which was played in England at the time and involved hitting a ball with a stick.

Around the same time that the window appeared in Gloucester, there was reference to the game of *chole* in Flanders in 1353. It was a long-distance cross country game played by two people who each had to hit a ball, with a club, towards a fixed target, which may have been a wall, a tree, door etc., depending on local terrain. This certainly resembled golf by virtue of the fact that it was played across

country. But other similar games had been played in Holland (*kolfspel*) and France (*jeu de maille*). And let's not forget the Romans played a game *paganica* which resembled golf.

But it is to Scotland we look further for origins of this great game.

LEFT: *The Crecy Window at Gloucester Cathedral was installed in the mid-14th century. A man can be seen swinging what appears to be a golf club.*

ABOVE: *Mary Queen of Scots was a keen sportswoman and enjoyed a game of golf. She is seen here at St Andrews in 1563.*

In 1457, the game of *gouf* suffered a similar fate to football when an edict was placed on it by an Act of Parliament banning it in Scotland. These two games, gouf and football, were taking men away from archery practice which was vital to the nation's defense particularly as attack from England to the south was a very real possibility at that time. Similar edicts followed in 1470 and 1491 in the times of King James III and James IV respectively.

Eleven years after imposing his ban on *gouf* James IV had a change of heart and actually acquired a set of clubs which were made for him by a Perth bowmaker. The King played golf regularly with the Earl of Bothwell and it was after engaging in a stakes match with Sir Robert Maule that Maule became the first golfer to be mentioned by name when he was so described in the *Panmure Register*. Their match took place at the Barry Links on the site of an 11th century battle between the Scots and Danes. This spot was close to the present-day Carnoustie course. By now golf was known as *gowf* and all the above evidence is thus leaning towards Scotland's claim to golf's birthright.

No matter which country claims to be the 'father' of golf, there is little doubting Scotland's claim to being the 'home' of golf. This claim was further substantiated in 1552 when the Archbishop of St Andrews granted the local community permission to play golf over the links of St Andrews.

Mary Queen of Scots became a lover of golf, just as she did many other sports, notably billiards, and in 1567 she came in for a fair amount of criticism for playing golf at Seton House within a couple of weeks of the death of her husband, Darnley, thus also adding fuel to the belief that she had organised his murder.

Golf was now becoming so popular in Scotland that edicts were no longer imposed by Parliament. However, the Church authorities were not pleased that so many people were engaging in this new pastime. And the playing of golf at Leith on Sundays was banned because too many people were neglecting church services.

In the early part of the 17th century the Prince of Wales was reported to have played golf at Greenwich (c.1607). It was the first mention of golf in England, the sport presumably having been brought

ABOVE: *A painting from 1674 by the Flemish artist Paul Bril depicting men playing the game of* mail à la chicane, *probably near Rome.*

RIGHT: *A painting by an unknown artist, c.1595. Some sources believe the model may have been Prince Henry, the eldest son of King James VI of Scotland.*

south by members of the Scottish royal court at the time of the union of the Scottish and English crowns in 1603. It was certainly the sport of the gentry in those days and the Marquis of Montrose followed his father's footsteps and played golf. The Marquis is believed to have been one of the first golfers to employ a caddie. His accounts for 1628 showed an entry of four shillings payable 'To the boy who carried my clubs'. And it was while playing golf at Leith in 1641 that King Charles received news from a messenger of a rebellion in Ireland. It is not known whether he 'did a Francis Drake' and carried on playing!

By now golf was definitely established in England and in 1658 there was mention of golf being played in London, at Upfields in Westminster. There's hardly enough room to swing a club in Westminster these days, let alone find space to lay out a golf course.

But the spread of golf led, in 1682, to the first international match when the Duke of York and a shoemaker (representing Scotland) challenged two noblemen of England over the Leith course (but not on a Sunday!). Matches took the form of stakes matches and in 1724 Alexander Elphinstone, the younger son of Lord Balmerino, and Captain John Porteous of the Edinburgh City Guard, played for a stake of 20 guineas (£21.05) at Leith. The match aroused a great deal of interest because of the size of the prizemoney on offer and consequently a big crowd turned out to watch.

Because of the large number of people playing golf it became necessary to formulate some rules. Previously, players had presumably agreed on common rules before each match but in 1744 the first rules of golf were drawn up following the formation of the

Honourable Company of Edinburgh Golfers. The Honourable Company is widely regarded as the world's first golf club and they formed themselves to play for a silver club donated by the City of Edinburgh. Local surgeon John Rattray was the first winner of the famous trophy. Formed on 1 May 1744 as the Gentlemen Golfers of Edinburgh, they played over five holes at Leith and it was decided that the winner of the silver trophy (to be contested annually) should hold the title 'Captain of the Golf' and that he, with help from other members, should settle all disputes concerning golf, whether they be at Leith or any other course. This led to the formulating of the first Rules of Golf.

When the forerunner of the Royal and Ancient Golf Club (of St Andrews) was founded ten years later their first set of rules was almost identical to that of the Gentlemen Golfers of Edinburgh, who,

in 1795, were granted permission to change their name to the Honourable Company of Edinburgh Golfers. They later moved their headquarters to Musselburgh and in 1891 to their present home at Muirfield.

By the mid 18th century golf was becoming an organised sport although it would be another century before the world's first major tournament would be inaugurated. Nevertheless, the sport was starting to produce its own characters and champions and we will be looking at them more closely as we continue our journey through the golfing years.

We said at the beginning that golf's birthright is uncertain, and it is, but like many other writers and historians, I am prepared to give Scotland the benefit of the doubt. Most people accept Scotland as the 'home' of golf. Why should we try to change that? There is no doubting the Scots' vast contribution to the development of golf as a sport. And that contribution should never be forgotten.

BELOW: *William Inglis on Leith Links, painted by David Allan in 1784. Inglis was Captain of the Gentlemen Golfers of Edinburgh in that year.*

THE BIRTH OF ST ANDREWS

Ten years after the formation of the Gentlemen Golfers of Edinburgh twenty two gentlemen 'being admirers of the anticient and healthfull exercise of the Golf' formed themselves into the Society of St Andrews Golfers. The twenty two men were noblemen, professional men, and professors, and they adopted the rules as laid down by their Leith counterparts. The devotees formed their society on 12 May 1754 and met at the Club House, the site of which is unknown. But it is known they fed themselves at Baillie Glass's before moving to the Union Parlour. The present club house was not erected until 1854, one hundred years after the formation of the Society. The club changed its name to the Royal and Ancient Golf Club in 1834 after gaining permission from King William IV who agreed to become the club's first captain, one of the most prestigious honors in golf.

The first rules adopted by the St Andrews' golfers were more or less the same as those adopted by the Honourable Company of Edinburgh Golfers but in 1759 the St Andrews Society had introduced rules governing stroke play. Previously all matches were of a match-play nature.

With the Honourable Company of Edinburgh golfers having to face an upheaval and move to Musselburgh, the Royal and Ancient Club became the more popular and it was to them that golfers turned for clarification of rules and in 1897 they officially became the governing authority on the rules of golf. They still hold that title today although the USGA does have its own variations. However, all major rule changes are done in collaboration with the R & A. Most other countries play to the Rules of Golf as laid down by the Royal and Ancient Club.

ABOVE RIGHT: *One of the best known sights in golf. The 18th green and clubhouse at St Andrews.*

ABOVE: *The trophy cabinet at St Andrews showing (above) the famous silver club first won by William Landale in 1754.*

RIGHT: *The Old Course at St Andrews, one of the most famous golf courses in the world. A good view of the undulating fairways of a classic links course.*

By the la' Harry
This shall not go for Nothing

COCK OF THE GREEN.

been connected with Prestwick although he was born at St Andrews). And in 1868 his son Tom junior made it a notable double for both family and the famous links. When St Andrews staged its first Open in 1873 the winner was Tom Kidd, a home player, and since then the 'home' of golf has produced some memorable championships and champions.

The nostalgic value of St Andrews makes it the most famous golf course in the world and you have only to play the Old Course to realise you are playing on a piece of golfing history.

ABOVE LEFT: *The style may have been different 200 years ago but the object was the same. The illustration shows Alexander McKellar, a well-known Edinburgh character from around 1800, who was so obsessive in his devotion to the game that he even played in the dark by lantern light.*

ABOVE: *A wonderful canvas by Charles Lees (1800-80) depicting the action and festivities at a 19th century golf match.*

ABOVE RIGHT: *Members outside the present clubhouse at St Andrews which was opened in 1854.*

The town of St Andrews dates to the 8th century and its University is the oldest in Scotland, dating to 1413. Golf was certainly played in the town long before the formation of the Society of St Andrews Golfers. There is evidence, for example, that Archbishop John Hamilton issued a license for golf to be played in St Andrews in 1552.

The original course, along St Andrews Bay, had 12 'greens'. However, a round consisted of 22 holes. The golfers started by playing from alongside the 'Home hole' (effectively the 22nd, but they did not play it at that stage) and played the 11 holes until reaching the far end of the course. They then turned and re-played the holes in the opposite direction before finishing at the home hole.

The first four holes were later reduced to two thus giving the course ten greens and making a round of 18 holes. Because of the increased number of players, golf at St Andrews became dangerous with players going in both directions at the same time. Consequently there was a need to widen the fairways and cut two holes into the huge greens. These 'double greens' remain a feature of the Old Course today.

A second course, the New Course was constructed in 1894. It is situated to the east of the Old Course. The Jubilee course was completed in 1899 and in 1912 the Eden course was laid out either side of the railway. The following year green fees were charged to members and visitors for the first time on the Old Course. It had been anticipated that playing golf at St Andrews would be free but the sheer volume of golfers in the early part of the 20th century necessitated such action. The four links at St Andrews are all municipal courses.

The Old Course has been the home of most of the great golf championships. It has staged the British Open 23 times, a figure second only to Prestwick, and St Andrews has produced many of golf's great champions, the first being Allan Robertson in the mid 19th century. His family had spent years as ballmakers at St Andrews but he was the first of the Robertsons to develop into an outstanding player.

In the early days of the Open championship, Andrew Strath was the first St Andrews player to make an impact and was the winner at Prestwick in 1865. Two years later the great Tom Morris senior became the second St Andrews winner of the title (previously he had

RIGHT: *'The Golfers' at St Andrews in 1847. This was originally a painting by Charles Lees and later a coloured engraving by Charles E Wagstaffe.*

PRE-CHAMPIONSHIP DAYS

In the days before the birth of the first great championship, the British Open in 1860, golf had been played by noblemen. Because of the increased popularity there became a demand for experienced club and ball makers. However, these craftsmen soon became the artisans of golf and it was not long before they had a better knowledge and understanding of the game than their more esteemed customers.

The matches that attracted big crowds to the likes of North Berwick, Musselburgh and St Andrews in those days, were those between nobility and gentry, or anybody who could afford to play for a sum large enough to make the match attractive. But the public soon realised that for watching skilful players they had to turn to the equipment manufacturers who had developed greater skills. These men became the forerunners of the professionals of today.

Because of transport difficulties, challenge matches often involved players from one club, or from adjoining clubs. Matches normally took place in foursomes.

The first great champion was Allan Robertson, son of a St Andrews ball-maker. Born at St Andrews on 11 September 1815, he holds the distinction of being the first golfer to break 80 over the 18 holes at St Andrews and is reputed never to have lost a match at foursomes or singles off level handicaps.

He engaged in one of the great money-matches of the pre-championship days when he and his assistant Tom Morris (snr) challenged the Dunn twins, Jamie and Willie, of Musselburgh in 1849.

Robertson and Old Tom were favorites for the match played at three courses, each over 36 holes. St Andrews and Musselburgh were the first two venues with the deciding 36 holes to be held at North Berwick.

Robertson and Morris won over their own course, while the Dunns

BELOW: *Old Tom Morris (holding flag stick) and Freddie Tait playing out in front of the Royal and Ancient clubhouse at St Andrews c.1895. Tait was an outstanding amateur of the day and excelled at rugby and cricket as well as golf.*

ABOVE: *This is what a Scottish caddie looked like in the first half of the 19th century. There were no luxuries like bags and trolleys.*

ABOVE RIGHT: *The greatest golfer of the pre-championship days, Allan Robertson of St Andrews.*

BELOW: *A group of golfers playing out of a bunker, possibly Hell Bunker, at St Andrews. This*

photograph was taken c.1860; championship golf was not far away.

had an emphatic 12 and 11 win at Musselburgh. In the decider at North Berwick Robertson and Morris found themselves trailing by four holes but remarkably they recovered to win by two holes.

Following a disagreement over the new 'gutta' ball they severed their business relationship. Old Tom moved on to Prestwick but they continued their allegiance on the golf course and became an invincible duo. Robertson was also innovative and was responsible for the use and development of iron clubs for delicate shots around the greens. Previously most clubs were wooden.

Willie Dunn, one of Robertson's rivals in that memorable 108-hole match, took over at the Royal Blackheath Club south of the border in 1844 and on one occasion played in a challenge match with Sir Robert Hay for the sum of £200. Dunn's salary at Blackheath at the time was a mere ten shillings (£0.50) per week.

Another notable family to follow Robertson's move and become 'professionals' were the Straths; Andrew, David and George. They were born at St Andrews but spread their skills across Scotland. David moved to North Berwick, Andrew to Prestwick, and George became Troon's first professional. He was also one of the first Scottish professionals to make the trip across the Atlantic as the golfing word was being spread into the United States.

Following the death of Robertson in 1859, golf's first champion was gone. There was a need to find his successor, and that was done by means of a tournament. And so was born the British Open the following year.

In the years leading up to the founding of the Open, Willie Park senior of Musselburgh and Old Tom Morris of Prestwick, were constantly competing with each other in an effort to establish superiority. Their chance to decide who should succeed Robertson as golf's 'champion' came in 1860, and the honour went to Park.

SPREADING THE GOLFING GOSPEL

Following the formation of the Honourable Company of Edinburgh Golfers and the St Andrews club, golf took great strides forward and by the end of the 18th century other clubs were being established, not only in Scotland, but elsewhere in Britain and across the Atlantic.

Other well known golf clubs to be established in Scotland were the Aberdeen Club in 1780, the Crail Golfing Society in 1786, and the Bruntsfield Society in 1787. Rumor has it that the Bruntsfield club was formed by members of the Edinburgh Burgess Society who, being strong supporters of the exiled Prince Charles Edward Stuart, and opponents of George III, would not drink a toast to the Hanoverian King at the Burgess Club. Consequently they broke away to form their own club. The Edinburgh Burgess (originally the Edinburgh Golfing Society and later the Royal Burgess Golfing Society of Edinburgh) is believed to have been formed in 1735 and can therefore lay claim to being the oldest continuously-existing golf club in the world, even dating before the Honourable Company and the Royal and Ancient Club.

LEFT: *The medal of the Edinburgh Burgess Golfing Society which claims to be the oldest golf club in the world, dating to 1735.*

LEFT: *'The Blackheath Golfer'. Engraved in 1778 by Lemuel Abbott, this is the earliest English depiction of golf or a golfer. The golfer is believed to be William Innes, captain of the Blackheath club at the time.*

By the time golf had taken a grip of Britain in the mid 19th century there had been mention of ladies playing golf when a tournament for fishwives was held at Musselburgh in 1810. And south of the border golf was not restricted to the Home Counties around London. The Old Manchester Club was formed at Kersal Moor in 1818. Within a few years, there came about three of the most famous courses in Scotland. Perth was formed in 1824, North Berwick in 1832 and in 1851 the Prestwick club was founded.

North Berwick was the scene of some of the great challenge matches in the pre-championship days and Prestwick, of course, was to be home to the first ever British Open in 1860.

In 1857 the first book of golf instruction, known as *The Golfer's Manual* was written by H B Farnie using the pseudonym 'A Keen Hand.' It highlighted the growing interest in the sport.

Although we have looked at the development of golf in Scotland, and occasionally England, the sport was being spread to wider horizons. In 1829 the Calcutta Golf Club was founded in India to make it the first club outside Britain. It later became the Royal Calcutta Club. India was the first location outside Britain where golf was taken seriously and several clubs were established. The original Calcutta Club was at Dum Dum, a north-east suburb of Calcutta, and now the site of the city's airport. The present course is at Toliganj. Thirteen years after the formation of the Calcutta Club the Bombay Golfing Society was formed to confirm India as a 19th century stronghold of golf.

Ireland got its first club in 1856 with the founding of the Curragh Club (later Royal Curragh) in County Kildare. And the same year the continent of Europe had its first club when the Pau Club in France was formed.

The golf word was being spread and while inroads were being made into Ireland, India and France, the United States was getting its first taste of this new pastime. Little did the Americans know at the time that within little over half a century they would dominate the world of golf and their country would be the home to more golf courses and golfers than the rest of the world put together.

Inevitably golf was introduced to the Americans by the Scots. Golf clubs and balls are known to have been imported from Scotland in the 1740s. And Scottish officers also played golf on American soil, near New York, during the Revolutionary War in 1779. But there was no continuity and even after the South Carolina Golf Association

ABOVE: *Opposing teams from the Brookline Country Club, Massachusetts and the Royal Montreal Club outside the Montreal clubhouse before the start of their first match in 1898.*

BELOW: *A plan showing the first two courses at St Andrew's, Yonkers. The first was a 3-hole course at John Reid's cowpasture. It was laid out in February 1888.*

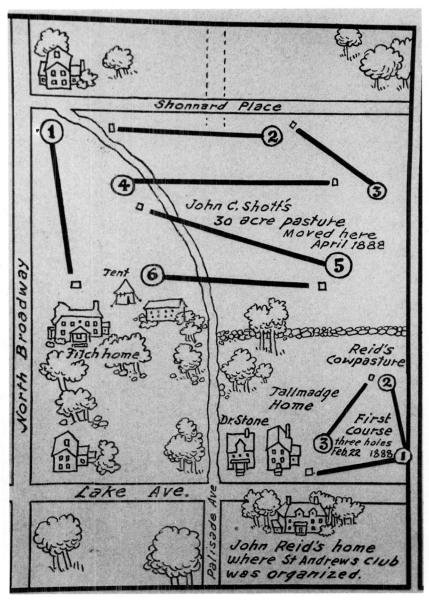

formed itself at Charleston in 1786, and golf was played at Savannah, Georgia, in 1795, there were no signs of the sport developing and expanding across the country and these clubs soon folded.

Another attempt to popularise golf was tried by members of the Oakhurst Golf Club at White Sulphur Springs, Virginia, in 1884 but again it was failure. It was now over 100 years since golf had first come to America and still it had not taken off. In Britain it was spreading at an alarming rate and in 1860 the British Open had been born. But the Americans had still not taken to the game. However, in the late 1880s it all changed and the golf 'boom' began across the Atlantic.

The Foxburg Club, Pennsylvania, was formed in 1887. They claim golf was played there two years earlier although there is no documented evidence to substantiate that claim. The Dorset Field Club, Dorset, Vermont, claims, also without documentation, to have played golf since 1886. These two clubs both claim to be the oldest continuously-existing club in America, but as no real documentation exists, their claims must be doubted. However, a third claimant is the St Andrew's Club of Yonkers, New York. Their history is well documented. The club was formed on 14 November 1888, although there is firm evidence of golf being played over their Yonkers course on 22 February that year.

In 1889 the Middlesboro Club in Kentucky was founded, and two years later came Shinnecock Hills, Long Island, named after the Indian tribe who once had their settlement at the far end of Long Island. By the end of the century there were one thousand courses across the United States as golf fever gripped the American public.

Many Scottish professionals, and ball and club makers, made the long trip across the 'pond' to take up similar posts at American clubs and by the time championship golf came to the United States at the end of the century, there was more than a sprinkling of Scottish presence among the list of champions.

Although golf spread rapidly once it had taken a grip in the USA, America was not the only country to see golf as a growth sport.

Australia's first club, the Adelaide Club (later Royal Adelaide) was formed in 1870 and the following year organised golf came to New Zealand at Dunedin and then to Christchurch. Like America, it did not endure at first, but it returned with a flourish in 1891 and has been popular in New Zealand ever since. Golf also reached Canada and the first club, the (Royal) Montreal Club was established in 1873. And in 1885 South Africa had its first golf club, albeit a six-hole course at Royal Cape.

By the end of the 19th century golf was being played in Belgium, Germany, Sweden, Denmark, the Canary Islands, Malaysia, Hong Kong, Thailand, Argentina, Mexico, and Rhodesia.

Inspired by the British Open and British Amateur Championship (inaugurated 1885) competitive golf came to most golf-playing nations. It was not just a pastime for the rich. There was the opportunity for the best players, amateur or professional, to show off their skills and talents in tournament play.

Golf had come a long way since the start of the 19th century. It was now ready to explode into one of the most popular participant sports of the 20th century. But even those golfers at the turn of the century could never have imagined what lay in store.

ABOVE LEFT: *Newport Golf Club, Rhode Island, in the late 19th century. It was the home of the first US Open in 1895. The quality of greens has improved considerably since then, thankfully!*

ABOVE: *Carnoustie in the late 1890s. The club had been officially opened nearly one hundred years before it staged the British Open for the first time, in 1931.*

RIGHT: *Lady golfers enjoying a round at Shinnecock Hills, Long Island. The course is named after the tribe of Indians who once had their settlement nearby.*

19

THE FIRST OF THE GREAT CHAMPIONSHIPS
THE BRITISH OPEN

Allan Robertson was widely acknowledged as the finest golfer of his day. Reportedly unbeaten at singles off a level handicap, and never beaten at foursomes, the more common type of match at the time, he was the truly outstanding player of his era. When Robertson died of jaundice at the age of 44 in 1859, there were several other golfers claiming to be successors to his 'crown', among them Old Tom Morris, Willie Park, Andrew Strath and Bob Andrew. The best way to decide the new 'champion of golf' was to hold a competition.

The Prestwick Club, although its course is sadly now no longer severe enough to qualify as a championship venue, was popular for challenge and stake matches in the mid-1800s. The course was laid out on common land and had opened in 1851. In 1857 Prestwick had succeeded in getting eight clubs to take part in a knockout tournament. When you think of the transport and communication difficulties almost one hundred and fifty years ago, arranging such a tournament was no mean feat. But the Prestwick Club were well organised and got the tournament off the ground. The following year they also arranged a tournament for amateurs. So, when the idea of a professional tournament was mooted, Prestwick was the obvious choice both for its golf course and ability to organise such an event.

It was thanks to a suggestion from Major J. O. Fairlie that the Open was instituted. And on Wednesday 17th October 1860 the first British Open Championship took place over three rounds of Prestwick's 12 hole course.

Just eight professionals took part in the first championship and the honor of becoming the first Open champion, and successor to Allan Robertson, fell to Musselburgh's Willie Park. The full scores of the eight competitors show a remarkable gap between the leading players and the 8th man:

174 **Willie Park**
   (Musselburgh)
176 **Tom Morris, Snr**
   (Prestwick)
180 **Andrew Strath**
   (St Andrews)
191 **Bob Andrew**
   (Perth)
192 **Daniel Brown**
   (Blackheath)
195 **Charles Hunter**
   (Prestwick St Nicholas)
196 **Alex Smith**
   (Bruntsfield)
232 **William Steel**
   (Bruntsfield)

LEFT: *The British Open championship medal presented to Willie Park (Jnr) after his one stroke win over Bob Martin at Prestwick in 1887. Park is said to have sent the medal back in disgust because it was so cheaply made.*

ABOVE: *Willie Park (Snr) of Musselburgh, the winner of the first British Open at Prestwick in 1860. Park beat Old Tom Morris by two strokes in a competition designed to find a successor to the late Allan Robertson's title as 'champion' of golf.*

Although called the 'Open' it was not strictly an Open event in its first year because it was limited to professionals only. However, the following year, following complaints from amateurs, it became a true Open event and has been ever since. Purists also insist that the correct title of the tournament is 'The Open Championship' without the word 'British' but this book will follow the more common usage and refer to the British Open.

The winner of the early tournaments received a championship belt. It was made out of red Moroccan leather and was presented by the Earl of Eglinton. When Young Tom Morris won the title for a third successive year in 1870 he was allowed to retain the belt permanently and because there was no trophy the following year there was no Open! However, it was revived in 1872 when the Prestwick Club asked the St Andrews Club and the Honourable Company of Edinburgh Golfers to share the cost of buying a new trophy, and also share the organisation, which they did. The new trophy was the magnificent claret jug which is still presented to the winner every year, and is the most sought after trophy in golf.

All championships up to 1870 had been held at Prestwick. But from 1872 the venue was shared in rotation between St Andrews, Prestwick, and Musselburgh. It was not until 1892 that another course, Muirfield, was used, but that was the new home of the

ABOVE: *A golfing diploma to mark the 50th anniversary of the British Open. It depicts the previous winners of the championship and spotlights the 'Great Triumvirate' of Braid, Taylor and Vardon.*

RIGHT: *Willie Fernie, British Open winner at Musselburgh in 1883 when he beat the local player Bob Ferguson in a play-off. Fernie, then of Dumfries and later of Felixstowe and Troon, was an excellent teacher of the game.*

Honourable Company of Edinburgh Golfers at the time. The Open was played outside Scotland for the first time in 1894 when it was held at Sandwich. All British Open courses are links courses and as at the end of 1989 only 14 different courses had been used. Prestwick and St Andrews have, by far, been used more times than the other 12.

The British Open was the forerunner of all other tournaments and despite its longevity remains the world's premier golf tournament and the one all professionals would dearly love to win. Some like Tony Lema in 1964 came and conquered. While others like the great Dai Rees could never quite win the coveted trophy. But the Open has produced many wonderful champions, all of whom will be mentioned in greater detail later in this book.

The first of the great champions was Tom Morris senior. He won the title four times. He was succeeded by his son, Young Tom who, in 1868, recorded the first hole in one at the Open when he had an ace at Prestwick's 8th hole. The Open's first winner, Willie Park also won the title three more times and in the period from the end of the 19th century to the First World War the triumvirate of Braid, Taylor and Vardon had a virtual monopoly on the championship winning it 16 times from 1894 to 1914.

The Americans made their big breakthrough in 1921 when Jock Hutchison took the trophy across the Atlantic for the first time. Since then, British golfers have had their work cut out to keep the trophy on British soil. And what a difficult task they've had with the likes of

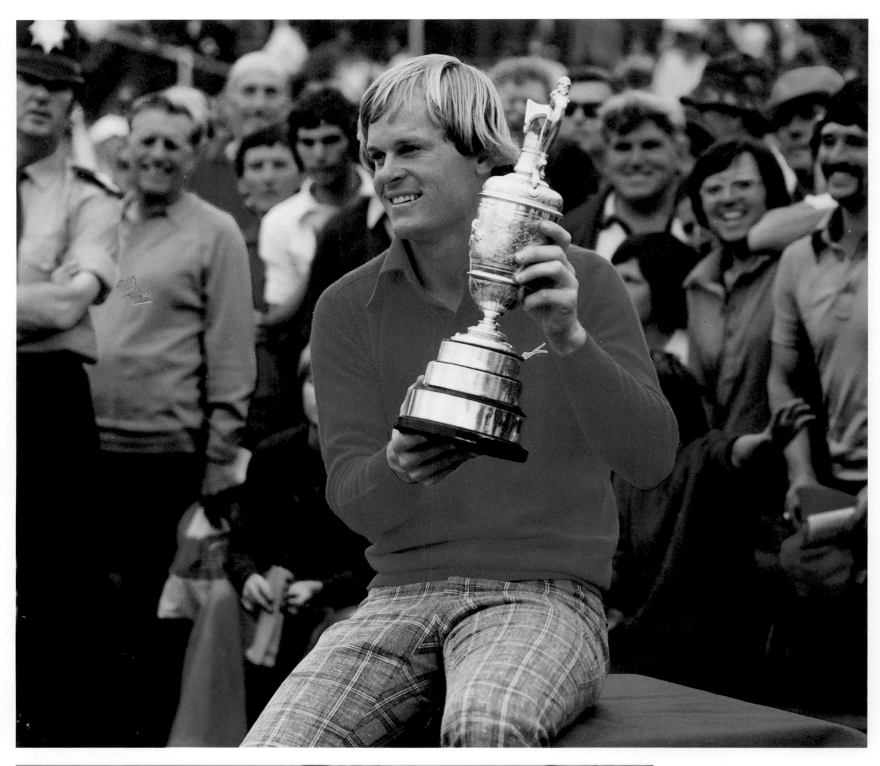

ABOVE: *One of the many 'Golden Boys' to have made the trip across the Atlantic and captured the British Open title: Johnny Miller, the 1976 winner at Royal Birkdale.*

LEFT: *'Champagne Tony' Lema, like every other winner, is clearly delighted by his British Open success. His win at St Andrews in 1964 was on the first occasion he entered the Open.*

Bobby Jones, Walter Hagen, Gene Sarazen, Ben Hogan, Sam Snead, Arnold Palmer, Jack Nicklaus, and Tom Watson to contend with. But there have been isolated pockets of home-based success thanks to Henry Cotton, Max Faulkner, Tony Jacklin, Sandy Lyle and Nick Faldo.

But how different it all is today with hundreds of competitors taking part in pre-qualifying rounds before the 72 hole competition proper in front of many thousands of fans, not to mention the millions more who watch on television.

Golf has come a long way since that October day at Prestwick in 1860 when only a few spectators watched the eight professionals trudge around 36 holes at an average of more than five shots per hole. But their scoring is irrelevant. They were the pioneers in what has become the finest golf tournament in the world. Prestwick, although not used for the Open since 1925, must never be forgotten either. It must always remain in the memory of all those golf fans as the home of the British Open. Without Prestwick there probably would not have been an Open in the first place.

LEFT: *Britain has had all too little success in her 'own' championship in recent years. But Sandy Lyle in 1985 and Nick Faldo (seen here) two years later have helped to rectify the situation.*

BELOW: *Tom Watson (right) and Jack Newton before their play-off to decide the 1975 Open champion. Watson won by one stroke from the unlucky Newton and it was to be the first of five successes for Watson who equalled the post-war record of Peter Thomson of Australia.*

THE MORRISES – YOUNG & OLD TOM

Successful father and son combinations in golf are a rarity these days. Gary and Wayne Player and Jack and Jacky Nicklaus are perhaps the best known examples today. But sadly the sons of those two illustrious golfers are not likely to match the successes of their fathers.

In the early days of championship golf however, successful father and son pairings were common. Willie Park senior and junior both won the British Open as did the Morrises, Young and Old Tom, the most successful father and son combination the world of professional golf has ever known.

Old Tom was born at St Andrews in 1821 and was one of the game's first real greats. He started playing golf at the age of six and at 15 became an apprentice ball-maker to Allan Robertson.

Robertson was widely regarded as the finest golfer of the day and when he and Old Tom teamed up to play in challenge matches they were invincible. Old Tom is believed to have twice beaten Robertson in unofficial matches at singles; quite a feat against a man who is reputed never to have lost an official singles match in his life. Because Robertson could see the alarming improvement of his protegé, he refused to meet Morris on level terms in a money match, much to the annoyance of Morris' backers.

A disagreement between Morris and Robertson over the new gutty ball which was introduced in 1848, led to them severing their business partnership although they continued to play together in challenge matches.

Morris went his own way for a while before accepting the post of custodian at the newly formed Prestwick links in 1851, the year his son, Young Tom was born.

Following the death of Robertson in 1859, many believed Old Tom his successor but the newly-inaugurated British Open was designed to see who was the champion. Tom missed out on the chance to put

ABOVE: *Young and Old Tom (both left) playing a challenge match in November 1875. A month later Young Tom tragically died of a broken heart at the age of 24.*

RIGHT: *Old Tom Morris, four times winner of the British Open and one of the most respected professionals in the early days of championship golf.*

his name in the record books when he was beaten by two strokes by Willie Park of Musselburgh. But the following year, 1861, Tom won the first of his four titles, the last being in 1867, two years after he returned to St Andrews as greenkeeper. He held that post until his retirement in 1904, and then in an honorary capacity until his death in 1908 at the age of 87. He played in every British Open from 1860-96, the last when he was 75 years of age. When he won his last title in 1867 he was 46 years 99 days old, the oldest winner of the title to this day. He would surely have added more titles to his name had it not been for the arrival of a brilliant newcomer on the professional golf scene, his son Young Tom.

Like his father, Young Tom was also born in St Andrews and also started swinging a club at an early age. Unlike his father though, Young Tom set out to be a tournament professional as opposed to a club professional. He appeared in his first British Open, at Prestwick in 1867, and finished 4th. He was just 16 at the time. That same year he beat Willie Park and Bob Andrew in a play off to win a professional tournament at Carnoustie.

The following year he succeeded his father as champion when he became the youngest ever winner of the title at 17 years 5 months 8 days, an amazing golfing feat never likely to be surpassed. On his way to winning the title Young Tom also got into the record books by holing in one at the 166 yard 8th hole, the first ace in the British Open.

That Open success was to herald the start of a remarkable career

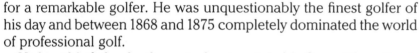

LEFT: *David Anderson's refreshment barrow at the 4th 'Ginger Beer' hole at St Andrews.*

ABOVE: *Young Tom Morris wearing the Open Championship Belt.*

RIGHT: *Young Tom's headstone at St Andrews Cathedral.*

for a remarkable golfer. He was unquestionably the finest golfer of his day and between 1868 and 1875 completely dominated the world of professional golf.

He beat his father by three strokes to retain his Open title at Prestwick in 1869 and the following year he won by 12 strokes with a score of 149 for the 36 holes. It would be nearly 35 years before scoring of that nature was to be seen again in the championship.

Young Tom became the permanent holder of the Open's championship belt after his third consecutive win in 1870 and consequently, there was no championship in 1871 because there was no prize. When it was revived in 1872 Young Tom was again the victor, by three strokes over David Strath. Morris was never to win the title again, although he finished second to Mungo Park at Musselburgh in 1874.

Although his style lacked the fluency of the modern-day golfer, he had immense power which was of great benefit in those days when the ability to thrash the ball out of the difficulties which abounded even on most fairways was much-needed. But he was a disciplinarian and set himself strict targets in practice. He would back himself to complete a round in 83 or less. He would win most times. To make the bet fairer he would then decrease his 'par' score. Invariably, he would continue to come out on the right side.

The golf world was deprived of one of its finest talents in 1875 when Young Tom Morris died at the age of 24.

While playing a challenge match with his father against Willie and Mungo Park at North Berwick in September 1875, Young Tom received a telegram saying his wife of barely a year was seriously ill during childbirth. He boarded a yacht and sped to his St Andrews home but it was too late. His wife and newborn baby had died. A bout of depression set in and he engaged in excessive drinking. On Christmas Day 1875 Young Tom Morris died, it is believed by some, of a broken heart.

Such was his standing at the time that 60 golfing societies around Britain contributed to the erection of a memorial in the cemetery at St Andrews Cathedral. The inscription on the headstone reads:

IN MEMORY OF
"TOMMY"
SON OF THOMAS MORRIS
WHO DIED 25th DECEMBER 1875 AGED 24 YEARS
•
DEEPLY REGRETTED BY NUMEROUS FRIENDS AND ALL GOLFERS
HE THRICE IN SUCCESSION WON THE CHAMPION'S BELT
AND HELD IT WITHOUT RIVALRY AND YET WITHOUT ENVY
HIS MANY AMIABLE QUALITIES
BEING NO LESS ACKNOWLEDGED THAN HIS GOLFING ACHIEVEMENTS
•
THIS MONUMENT HAS BEEN ERECTED
BY CONTRIBUTORS FROM SIXTY GOLFING SOCIETIES

Old Tom kept the family flag flying but that eventually came to an end when he retired in 1904 before his eventual death four years later. He outlived his son by 33 years. And who knows how many more British Open titles Old Tom would have won had Young Tom not appeared on the scene. And how many more Young Tom would have won had it not been for his untimely death. These are two questions that will never be answered. But their record of winning eight titles between them is remarkable enough. As a father and son pair, they are unquestionably the most successful ever seen in the world of professional golf.

PRESTWICK
THE RISE & FALL OF A GREAT COURSE

The golfing world owes a huge debt to the Prestwick Club. Situated on the Ayrshire coast of Scotland, it was Prestwick which gave us the first British Open championship back in 1860. Had it not been for the birth of that great championship, there is little doubting that championship golf the world over would not have existed in its present form.

Golf had been played in Prestwick for many years before the course was opened on common land in 1851. Its splendid turf was typical of such seaside courses and its feature of small greens hidden among undulating hollows around the course made it a testing layout even in those early days.

The first course consisted of 12 holes and it was three times over these 12 holes on 17 October 1860 that eight professionals competed in the first British Open Championship. The competition was organised solely by the Prestwick Club, as were all Opens until 1870, and from 1872 the responsibility was shared between Prestwick, the Honourable Company of Edinburgh Golfers and the Royal and Ancient club.

As we have seen Willie Park of Musselburgh was the winner of the first British Open but the following year Prestwick's own Tom Morris senior, won the championship by four strokes from Park. The early championships were dominated by Morris and Park and they shared the first five Opens between them before a St Andrews man, Andrew Strath got his name on the trophy. But Prestwick was soon to revel in the delights of the talented Young Tom Morris who won the Open

ABOVE: *The Prestwick club flag which is flown on match days.*

BELOW: *The 17th green at Prestwick which is approached by playing a blind shot over the 'Alps'.*

three years running from 1868-70. Prestwick staged every British Open from 1860-72 and thereafter shared the tournament in rotation with St Andrews and Musselburgh.

By the turn of the century other well known players had seen their names inscribed on the new British Open trophy after success at Prestwick, by that time an 18 hole layout after the addition of six extra holes in 1883. Jamie Anderson won the second of his three consecutive titles over the famous course in 1878, as did Bob Ferguson three years later. Willie Park junior followed in his father's footsteps and won the title at Prestwick in 1887. And in 1890 the great amateur of the day, John Ball of Royal Liverpool, beat Willie Fernie by three strokes to win the Open. He was the first English winner of the championship, and also the first amateur winner.

Ball won the first of his eight Amateur titles at Prestwick in 1888, the first time the course staged the Championship. Ball won his 5th title at Prestwick in 1899 when he beat defending champion Freddie Tait with a magnificent three at the 37th hole, the 1st, which runs alongside the railway line.

Harry Vardon won the Open three times at Prestwick, in 1898, 1903 and 1914, when he achieved his record breaking sixth title and another member of the 'Great Triumvirate', James Braid, had an eight stroke winning margin when he beat Tom Ball in 1908. It was fortunate for Braid that he had such a cushion because he took eight strokes in trying to get out of the treacherous Cardinal bunker on the 3rd hole. Despite this, his score of 291 lowered the 72 hole record for the championship by five strokes.

As the 1920s arrived and the American invasion started, Prestwick was no longer felt to be challenging enough for the new breed of pro-fessional golfer and in 1925 the British Open was played over one of golf's best known courses for the last time. The short closing holes, in particular, were no longer severe enough for such an event. In 1925 Jim Barnes maintained the American dominance of the championship with a one stroke victory over Ted Ray and Archie Compston. Barnes' fellow American Macdonald Smith threw away a five stroke lead in the final round to finish with an 82 and end up three shots behind the winner. As well as the doubts about the difficulty of the course, the popularity of the Open had seen crowds swell year-by-year, and Prestwick's geographical location made it difficult to control and marshal the influx of visitors. Furthermore the limited space for car parking and other amenities was no longer suitable for such an occasion and Prestwick disappeared from the British Open rota after staging the championship a record 24 times.

Just because the Open ceased to be played there it did not mean the end of Prestwick as a championship course. The Amateur championship was played there on various occasions until 1952. In fact one of the greatest displays of golf seen at the famous course was during the 1934 Amateur championship when Lawson Little destroyed Jock Wallace 14 and 13. Wallace was a local player and thousands of fans tried to make their way to the course. By the time many of them had arrived the American had completed his demolition job on the local hero.

Sadly, since 1952, when American Harvie Ward won the Amateur title, Prestwick has been used very little for senior championships but Prestwick has not been forgotten. Its place in golf's tradition makes it a popular stopping off point for golfing societies and for many a trip to Scotland would not be complete without a visit.

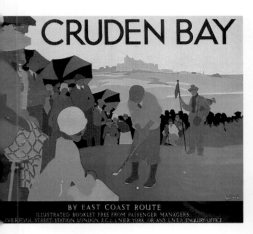

ABOVE: *By the 1930s, when this poster was produced, golfing holidays in Scotland were already popular. Cruden Bay is situated north of Aberdeen on Scotland's east coast.*

RIGHT: *Cruden Bay's 15th and 16th greens.*

ABOVE: *A British Railways poster advertising North Berwick, one of Prestwick's rival courses.*

RIGHT: *The 9th green at North Berwick's East links overlooks the North Sea.*

TOP LEFT: *One of golf's best known bunkers, the 'Cardinal Bunker' at Prestwick's 3rd hole.*

RIGHT: *Freddie Tait who lost a memorable Amateur championship final to John Ball at Prestwick in 1899. Ball won at the 37th hole. For the defending champion Tait it was to be his final championship before his untimely death the following year.*

FAR RIGHT: *Bob Ferguson of Musselburgh. He won the Open three years in succession 1880-82. His second success was by three strokes from Jamie Anderson at Prestwick.*

COMPETITIVE GOLF COMES TO THE USA

By the time of the 1890s golf was taking a grip on the US public. Courses were springing up and many Scottish immigrants were bringing their knowledge and skills across the Atlantic.

Competitive golf had existed in Britain since 1860 with the founding of the British Open. The first British Amateur Championship had been launched in April 1885, in 1893 the Ladies' British Open Amateur Championship was begun and by the end of 1894 the championships of New Zealand, Australia, India and Malaysia had been set up. It was only to be expected that American golfers would want their own championship and in 1895 they got not one but three.

The Amateur Golf Association of the United States was founded on 22 December 1894 with just five founder members and Henry O Tallmadge as its first secretary. The new association was formed because there was a lack of uniformity among the new clubs which had been opened and it was after two 'unofficial' Amateur championships of the United States had been run, one by the Newport Club, Rhode Island, and the other by the St Andrew's Club, Yonkers, New York, that Tallmadge, honorary secretary at St Andrew's, brought together interested member clubs at a dinner in New York with a view to forming an association.

One of the first tasks was to organise an official Amateur Championship and in 1895 the first US Amateur Championship was held over the 9-hole Newport, Rhode Island, course and was won by Charles Blair Macdonald, a former St Andrews (Scotland) student. He was succeeded as champion by his son-in-law H J Whigham the following year.

The Amateur championship opened the door for other championships in the United States and on 4 October 1895 the first official US

ABOVE: *Young Willie Dunn (middle of the back row) claimed to be the first US Open champion after winning an unofficial championship in 1894. Only four competitors took part. The following year he was runner-up in the first official championship which was held at Newport, Rhode Island.*

Open was played, also at Newport. Ten professionals and one amateur (A W Smith of Toronto) took part and the first champion was another exile, Englishman Horace Rawlins. He collected a cheque for $150 for his efforts. The Amateur Championship and Open were played in the same week and concurrently. They had been scheduled for the September but had to be put back because they clashed with the America's Cup yacht races around Rhode Island.

Not to be outdone by their male counterparts, the inaugural US Women's Amateur Championship was launched the same year to make 1895 a memorable year in US golfing history.

The new US Golf Association was tested to its fullest in 1896 when a 16 year old colored caddie named John Shippen entered the US Open at Shinnecock Hills. Several professionals threatened to boycott the event but the Association's president Theodore A Havemeyer dug in his heels and announced that Shippen would play and the tournament would take place with or without the protesting professionals. Shippen played, so did the protestors. Scottish professional Jim Foulis won the title and Shippen finished joint fifth.

The British influence on the Open in its early days was evident with either English or Scottish immigrants lifting the title. And in 1900 the trophy went out of the United States for the first time when Harry Var-

ABOVE LEFT: *Charles Blair Macdonald, the first winner of the US Amateur Championship in 1895.*

ABOVE: *H J Whigham was the second US amateur champion. He was the son-in-law of the first champion, Charles Blair Macdonald.*

LEFT: *Seated front is Horace Rawlins, the first official US Open champion in 1895 when he won over his home course at Newport. Also in the picture is Willie Anderson, the first man to win four US Open titles. He is seen behind Rawlins with his arm around Alex Smith who won the title in 1906 and 1910.*

don made the trip to the Chicago Club and beat his compatriot J H Taylor by two strokes.

In the early part of the 20th century there emerged an outstanding golfer in the shape of Willie Anderson. Formerly of the Pittsfield club and then Apawamis, he won his first US Open title at Myopia Hunt in 1901. He regained his title at Baltusrol in 1903 and won again in 1904 and 1905. To this day no other man has won the Open three years in succession. However Anderson was Scottish-born and the Americans were still waiting their first home-grown winner of the

championship. But they still had to wait a few more years.

Anderson's great run was ended by Alex Smith in 1906. Alec Ross, who, like Smith was born in Scotland, won the title in 1907 and the following year the champion was Fred McLeod, also a Scot, who weighed in at a mere 108 pounds, the smallest ever winner of the title, English-born George Sargent won the title in 1909 with a record low aggregate of 290 and the following year Alex Smith regained his title after a three way play off with Johnny McDermott and his own brother, Macdonald Smith.

RIGHT: *Willie Anderson, US Open champion in 1901 and 1903-05. He is the only man to win the title three years in succession and he was the first winner to develop his game in the United States.*

OPPOSITE PAGE: *Philadelphia-born Johnny McDermott became the first US born winner of the Open in 1911.*

BELOW: *Horace Rawlins beat a field of ten professionals and one amateur to capture the inaugural US Open in 1895. English-born he had arrived in the United States shortly before the tournament to become assistant at the Newport club, the hosts to the first championship.*

McDermott was born in Philadelphia and came close to becoming the first American-born winner of the US Open but in 1911 he gave the American golfing fans what they wanted when, this time, he emerged at the head of the pack after a three way play off. He retained his title in 1912 and in 1913 a little known 20 year old son of a coachman who lived across the street from the Brookline Country Club changed the course of golfing history, clearly ending the domination of British golfers on both sides of the Atlantic. The 'unknown' golfer was Francis Ouimet who came from obscurity to conquer the best of British golf in the shape of Harry Vardon and Ted Ray.

A record field of 170 gathered for the 1913 Open at Brookline, including many amateurs, and all were spurred on by the presence of the leading Britons. Qualifying became necessary and the two out-standing Britons qualified with ease and justified their positions as pre-championship favorites. The rest, including Ouimet were 'also rans.'

Ouimet had competed in the recent Amateur championship and fared well against the eventual winner Jerome Travers. He received rave reviews for his performance. But he could never have imagined what the next few days at Brookline had in store for him.

A drought during that summer meant that conditions favored long hitters. That was to Vardon and Ray's advantage. And Brookline's 150 bunkers demanded the best of skills. Again to the advantage of the two Britons.

The first 36 holes were completed on the first day and Vardon shared the lead with another fellow Briton, Wilf Reid, on 147. Ray was

two shots adrift and Ouimet was on 151. Sixes at the opening two holes cost the American a chance of the lead, or at least a share of it. Playing with the 1909 champion George Sargent, Ouimet started the first half of the second day with a 74 in one of the coolest displays of golf seen in the championship. Ray ended the third round with a 76 and Vardon was on 78. The leaderboard showed the two Britons level on 225 but they were accompanied by Francis Ouimet. 'Francis who?' asked many of the fans.

The final 18 holes were played in dreadful rain and there were few who really believed Ouimet would maintain his remarkable challenge. But he did, despite completing the first nine holes in 43. Vardon and Ray were finished and in the club-house sharing the lead on 304. Ouimet needed a 35 on the inward half to win, or 36 to get into a play off. At the 18th he had a 35-foot putt for the title. The ball rolled past the hole by three feet and he had an awkward return putt to share the lead. He made it and so he went into a three-way play off.

Despite Ouimet's charge, money was still being placed on Vardon and Ray. But those investors forgot to allow for the nerve of the

LEFT: *Francis Ouimet changed the course of golfing history with his memorable US Open win in 1913. Although not the first 'home' winner of the tournament, he was first to win against a field including the best British players of the day.*

RIGHT: *Ouimet with caddie.*

BELOW: *The young Ouimet (center) is being congratulated by the two fancied Britons Harry Vardon (left) and Ted Ray, after the youngster's amazing triumph in the play-off to win the 1913 Open.*

youngster from just over the road from the Brookline course. He had never once been intimidated, and during the play off remained as cool as he had done in the previous four rounds. The play off was over 18 holes and at the end of the first nine there had never been more than one stroke separating all three men. At the half-way stage they were all square on 38 each.

Ouimet struck the first blow at the 10th with a three and increased his lead to two shots by the 12th. It was back to one at the 13th. Going into the 17th Ray was out of it on 70. Vardon was on 66 and Ouimet on 65. At the end of the hole Ouimet held a three stroke lead over Var-

don and the Championship was all but won. Minutes later he was mobbed by thousands of admiring fans. No longer were they asking the question: 'Who's Francis Ouimet?' They knew only too well.

Ouimet's win ended the British dominance of world golf. Making his Open debut at Brookline was Walter Hagen, who was to be one of the first American superstars to dominate the game both in the United States and across the Atlantic. Francis Ouimet opened the door for American golf and since that memorable day at Brookline in 1913, US golfers have flooded through to stamp their authority on world golf.

GOLF'S FIRST GREAT TRIUMVIRATE
BRAID, TAYLOR & VARDON

Nicklaus, Palmer and Player were golf's outstanding trio in the sixties. In the forties and fifties it was Hogan, Nelson and Snead. But the first great golfing trio, known affectionately as 'The Great Triumvirate' was the threesome of Harry Vardon, James Braid, and John Henry (JH) Taylor.

They dominated British golf in the 20 years between 1894 and 1914 when they won 16 British Open titles between them. On top of that Vardon made the trip across the Atlantic and took the US Open crown in 1900.

Vardon was the most successful of the three, winning the Open six times, a record which still stands more than 75 years later. Born in 1870 at Grouville, Jersey, he was a caddie at his home course for some years but played very little golf. His brother Tom moved to England to become an assistant professional at St Anne's and suggested to Harry that he should make the same move and in 1890 the 20 year old moved to Ripon, North Yorkshire. After a year he moved

to Bury St Edmunds and in 1893 he made his British Open debut, but did nothing to attract any attention. The following year, however, he finished fifth and served notice that a great talent was about to unfold. And at Muirfield in 1896 Harry Vardon won the first of his record six titles.

Having moved to the famous Yorkshire Club, Ganton, he won the title by beating J H Taylor by four strokes in a 36 hole play off. When he won his second title at Prestwick two years later he beat the former champion Willie Park by one stroke after a final round 76. Title number three came in 1899 when he had a five stroke winning

BELOW: *The 'Triumvirate' from left to right: Harry Vardon, James Braid, J H Taylor. Seated is another former British Open champion Ted Ray. Between them the four men won 17 British Opens.*

RIGHT: *Braid, Taylor and Vardon as depicted in a 1917 oil painting by Clement Flower.*

JOHN HENRY TAYLOR
Open Champion
1894.1895.1900.1909.1913. *tied* 1896.

JAMES BRAID
Open Champion
1901.1905.1906.1908.1910.

HARRY VARDON
Open Champion
1896.1898.1899.1903.1911.1914.

CLEMENT
FLOWER
1913

margin over Jack White at Sandwich. Twelve months later Vardon was champion of the United States when he beat Taylor by two strokes at Chicago. More significantly, Vardon spent a year touring the United States and he did much to popularise the game on that side of the Atlantic.

In 1902 Vardon moved to the South Herts Club and the following year won his fourth British Open, and second at Prestwick, when he beat his brother Tom into second place. He spent some time in a sanatorium after that but came back to win his fifth Open at Sandwich when he beat the Frenchman Arnaud Massy in a play off. And three years later, at the age of 44 he won his sixth and last British Open when he beat Taylor by three strokes at Prestwick. In 1920, at the age of 50, he made another assault on the US Open, but was beaten into second place by Ted Ray after throwing away a six stroke lead with seven holes to play.

Harry Vardon stood only 5ft 9in tall but had great power and accuracy. He popularized the overlapping grip, which is commonly known as the 'Vardon Grip'.

Still the professional at South Herts up till the time of his death, Vardon died in 1937 at the age of 66.

Vardon was not however, the first member of the Triumvirate to win the British Open. That honor fell to John Henry Taylor, better

known as 'JH'. The son of a Devon laborer, he left school at the age of 11 with very little education. After a series of jobs he joined the green-keeping staff at Devon's famous Westward Ho! Golf Club. He turned professional at the age of 19 and moved to Burnham in nearby Somerset, where he became a greenkeeper. It is said that he left his Devon home with a borrowed sovereign to go searching for his fortune. He was later to find it.

Taylor soon moved to the Winchester Club and won his first British Open at Sandwich in 1894 when he beat Douglas Rolland by five strokes. It was the first playing of the Open outside Scotland. He retained his title the following year with a four stroke victory over Sandy Herd at St Andrews. It was also at St Andrews, in 1900, that Taylor won title number three when he had a remarkable eight stroke win over Vardon, with Braid in third place. By now Taylor was with the Mid Surrey Club, having joined them after a brief spell at Wimbledon. He spent the last 40 years of his career as professional at Mid Surrey.

It was not until 1909 that Taylor was to again re-assert his supremacy when he beat Braid by four strokes at Prestwick. His final moment of glory came at Hoylake in 1913 when he beat Ted Ray by eight shots to win the Open.

Taylor was a great competitor and in his later days refused to take part in a competition he thought he could not win. Away from the

LEFT: *Despite being 50 years of age Harry Vardon (right) was runner-up in the 1920 US Open at Inverness, Ohio, just one stroke behind the winner Ted Ray (second from left). The other competitors shown are Charlie Lorms, the Inverness pro, (left) and Deke White. Both finished well down the field.*

RIGHT: *Harry Vardon was the most successful of the Triumvirate. He won the British Open six times which still remains a record. This picture was taken in 1907 when he was 37 years of age.*

BELOW: *Harry Vardon made famous the overlapping grip which now bears his name and is still widely used.*

golf course he made up for his lack of education by reading a lot, and eventually turned to writing. He was also the instigator of the Professional Golfers' Association in 1901 as he sought to obtain a better deal for the professional. With his passing away in 1963 at the age of 92, it ended the last link between the great golfers from the turn of the century and those of today.

The third and final member of the Great Triumvirate was James Braid, the only Scottish-born member of the trio, who like Vardon, was born in 1870. The son of a ploughman, he left school at the age of 13 to become an apprentice joiner. He was then invited to London to become an apprentice club-maker for the famous Army and Navy Stores. He turned professional in 1893 and made his Open debut the following year, when Taylor won at Sandwich. An opening 91 ensured Braid would not be among the front runners. After moving to the Romford Club in the spring of 1896 he finished second to Harold Hilton at Hoylake in the 1897 Open.

His first British Open success came in 1901 when he beat Vardon and Taylor into second and third places respectively at Muirfield. Not naturally a long hitter of the ball, Braid found extra distance through sheer dedication to practice and over the next nine years he won the Open on four more occasions to become the first man to win the title five times.

FAR LEFT: *John Henry 'J H' Taylor won five British Opens with his short punchy swing.*

LEFT: *J H Taylor giving golf instruction at London's most famous store,* Harrods, *in 1914.*

BELOW LEFT: *James Braid – like Taylor he won the British Open on five occasions.*

BELOW: *Braid on his way to victory in the Jubilee Open at St Andrews in 1910. He won by four strokes from Sandy Herd.*

After finishing in second place in 1902 and 1904, when only one shot off the lead, he beat J H Taylor by five strokes to win his second title at St Andrews in 1905. Braid was by now the professional at Walton Heath. He retained his title at Muirfield a year later, with Taylor once more floundering in second place, this time four shots adrift. After letting Frenchman Arnaud Massy take the title in 1907 Braid regained it a year later with an eight stroke victory over West Lancashire's Tom Ball. His score of 291 was an Open record until bettered by Bobby Jones in 1927. Braid was runner-up once more, to Taylor in 1909 but the following year, at St Andrews, Braid made golfing history by winning his fifth Open.

After his competitive playing days, Braid was much sought after as a course designer and helped with the design, or re-design of such courses as Royal Blackheath Carnoustie, and Gleneagles. He died in 1950 and up to the time of his death was still an active member of the Walton Heath Club, where he had been a member since 1902. In the year of his death, Braid, along with J H Taylor and Willie Auchterlonie, was elected an honorary member of the R & A, the first professionals to receive such an honor.

IT'S NOT JUST A MAN'S GAME

By the time Francis Ouimet struck a blow for American golfers at Brookline, women golfers were already striking a blow for their sex and had established ladies golf in organised tournaments on both sides of the Atlantic.

Mary Queen of Scots paved the way for all women golfers by playing the game in the mid 16th century, and in 1810 those 'fishwives' of Musselburgh played in the first all-ladies competition. But since the latter part of the 19th century women's golf has become organised and today professional lady golfers earn money that their male counterparts would have been delighted to have earned a decade ago.

The first ladies golf club was formed at St Andrews in 1867 when normal Victorian day-wear, long skirts, tight fitting jackets, and, of course, a hat, were the attire of the lady golfer of the day. There was no such thing as a glimpse of leg.

The year after the formation of the St Andrews club, the first ladies club in England was formed, at Westward Ho! in Devon. Ladies golf became more organised in 1893 following the formation of the Ladies' Golf Union in Great Britain which resulted in the start of the British Ladies' Championship. Strictly for amateurs, the first winner was Lady Margaret Scott who beat Isette Pearson 7 & 5 at St Annes. Lady Margaret won the first three championships before handing over the title to Amy Pascoe in 1896.

A year after the British, Australian women followed the lead and started their own championship and in 1895 the US Women's Amateur Championship was launched and won by Mrs C S Brown with a score of 132 over 18 holes at Meadow Brook. Since that in-

BELOW: *This ladies putting tournament seems to be attracting a lot of interest! The venue is St Andrews in the late 1800s. The first lady golfers are believed to have been restricted to putting competitions because it was thought unseemly for a lady to attempt a full swing.*

augural championship which was stroke-play, all subsequent events have been held at match-play.

International golf matches between Great Britain and the United States have been regular occurrences for men (Walker Cup and Ryder Cup) and women (Curtis Cup) since the 1920s but the very first match between the two great golfing nations was in 1905 when The British Ladies defeated The American Ladies 6-1 at Cromer, England. In the US side that day were sisters Harriot and Margaret Curtis. Twenty seven years later they lent their name to the Curtis Cup.

Since the war, and notably since the 1970s, professional ladies golf has attained new heights, particularly in the United States. Sponsorship and large purses make the professional game an attractive proposition for the aspiring youngster, all wishing to emulate one or another of their own female heroes. And ladies golf has had its fair share of 'greats' over the years.

Britain's Lottie Dod, a former Wimbledon tennis champion won the British Open Amateur Championship in 1904. But the most outstanding British woman golfer in the pre-war days was Joyce Wethered (later Lady Heathcoat-Amory) who won the title four times. In the post-war years Britain has produced such notable champions as

RIGHT: *Lady Margaret Scott, the winner of the first three British Ladies Championships 1893-95.*

OVERLEAF: *Early lady golfers in action, from a magazine illustration of the 1890s.*

BELOW: *The four semi-finalists in the British Ladies Golf Championship at Portrush in 1895. Seated on the left is the eventual winner Lady Margaret Scott. She beat Miss E Lythgoe 3 and 2.*

THE MEDALISTS FOR THE GOLF CHAMPIONSHIP. PORTRUSH. /95. LEE. (H)

R. TAYLOR

ABOVE: *Britain's outstanding lady golfer in the inter-war years, Joyce Wethered. She won the English Ladies title four times in succession and the British title four times between 1922-29. Bobby Jones once commented after a round with her that he thought she was the best golfer, male or female, he had ever seen.*

LEFT: *Alexa Stirling (left) was one of the first great stylists of US women's golf. That probably came from the fact that she played a lot of her golf with an Atlanta neighbor – Bobby Jones. She won three successive US Women's amateur championships in 1916, 1919-20. On the right is Glenna Collet who won a record six US Women's titles between 1922-35. She was also runner-up for the British title on two occasions.*

Michelle Walker, Cathy Panton and Laura Davies, who shook the Americans by winning the US Women's Open in 1987. But for outstanding women golfers one must look to the American side of the Atlantic to find the true greats.

One of the truly outstanding lady golfers was Babe Zaharias, widely regarded as the finest all-round female sportswoman ever. Born as Mildred Didrikson, she married wrestler George Zaharias and became affectionately known as 'Babe' because of her baseball skills, reminiscent of those of the great Babe Ruth in the male game.

Zaharias won the Amateur golf championships of the US and Britain in 1946 and 1947 respectively and then won the US Women's Open three times between 1948 and 1954. All these triumphs came after she had collected two gold and a silver medal at the 1932 Olym-

pic Games in the javelin, 80 metres hurdles, and high jump. Furthermore, she was also an all-American basketball player. The year before her last Open win she had undergone cancer surgery, thus making her 12 stroke triumph a great emotional occasion. Sadly, she died in September 1956.

As the memory of the 'Babe' remained, two more great American lady golfers were emerging in the form of Mickey Wright and Kathy Whitworth who, during their long careers, went on to win more than 160 US Tour events. Since then there have been other such great stars of the US ladies game as JoAnne Carner, Nancy Lopez, Jan Geddes, Betsy King, Pat Bradley and Patty Sheehan. Patty Berg, the darling of US golf in the 1950s, won a record 15 women's majors, and close behind her total is Mickey Wright with 13.

ABOVE: *Harriot Curtis (left) and her sister Margaret. They were both excellent golfers and both won the US Women's National Amateur title. The Curtis Cup was their idea and they presented the trophy which was first contested in 1932.*

RIGHT: *One of the finest women golfers of all-time, 'Babe' Zaharias. As Mildred Didrikson she was an outstanding athlete before turning to golf, and won two gold medals at the 1932 Los Angeles Olympics.*

The US Women's Open is the leading event in women's golf and the other three major championships are currently the LPGA Championship, Nabisco Dinah Shore Classic, and the Du Maurier Classic.

There are millions of lady golfers worldwide, and the ladies game professionally enjoyed an upsurge in popularity and interest in the 1980s. The great stars of today are gaining just rewards for their talents. In return they provide the paying public with very fine golf indeed. Golf certainly isn't just a man's game.

47

THE CHANGING FACE OF GOLF EQUIPMENT

Athletes can run faster, jump higher and throw further than they used to. And racing drivers can speed around the Indianapolis Raceway far faster than they did eighty years ago. They both owe their improved performances in large part to technological advances. Golfers are no different. Consequently, because of such advances and improved equipment, they can play their game better. And that applies equally to the club player as to the professional.

Early golf was probably played with balls carved out of a piece of wood, and hit with a wooden club or stick. Can you imagine hitting a solid wooden ball? Furthermore, can you imagine how 'round' the ball would have been. There were no such things as precision tool makers in the 17th and 18th centuries.

Since the days of the wooden ball there have been three other widely used type of golf ball, all of which have, in turn, improved the standard of golf.

The first 'new' ball was the feathery which is believed to have first

ABOVE: *At least a top hat-full of feathers, normally goose feathers, was required to make one feathery ball. Understandably, because of the work involved, these balls were expensive.*

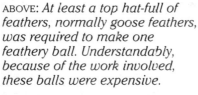

LEFT: *Robert Forgan in his club-making factory at St Andrews in the latter part of the 19th century. The Forgan family ran one of the best-known club- and ball-making businesses in the town for many years.*

been used in the 15th century and was so called because it was a stitched leather casing filled with feathers. Each ball was hand made and consequently not all balls were the same size, weight, or even shape!

The biggest technological advancement in golfing history came in 1848 when the Rev. Robert Preston invented the 'Gutty' ball. It was so called because it was made of gutta-percha, a brownish-red gum substance which came from Malaya. Although Preston is widely acknowledged as 'inventing' the gutty, credit for actually making the first ball goes to a member of staff of the golf ball manufacturers, W. T. Henley, who made the first gutty for use at the Blackheath Club.

For the first time golfers were given a choice of balls that were truly round because it was possible to mould the gutty. However, it didn't have any dimples like the modern-day golf ball. It had a flat surface and when struck it entered into a true flight. Nevertheless, it was a big improvement on the feathery.

One of the big problems with the gutty was its tendency just to 'fall' from the sky like a dead bird without completing its 'true' trajectory.

LEFT: *A selection of mid-19th century featheries. They certainly lacked uniformity of shape and size.*

FAR RIGHT: *The first golf bags were introduced around 1880 when it was becoming common for players to have six or more clubs.*

RIGHT: *The changing face of putters; all of these were classed as illegal and subsequently banned.*

LEFT: *An early wooden headed club, pre-1800.*

LEFT: *A long-nosed wood used in the day of the feathery and gutty balls.*

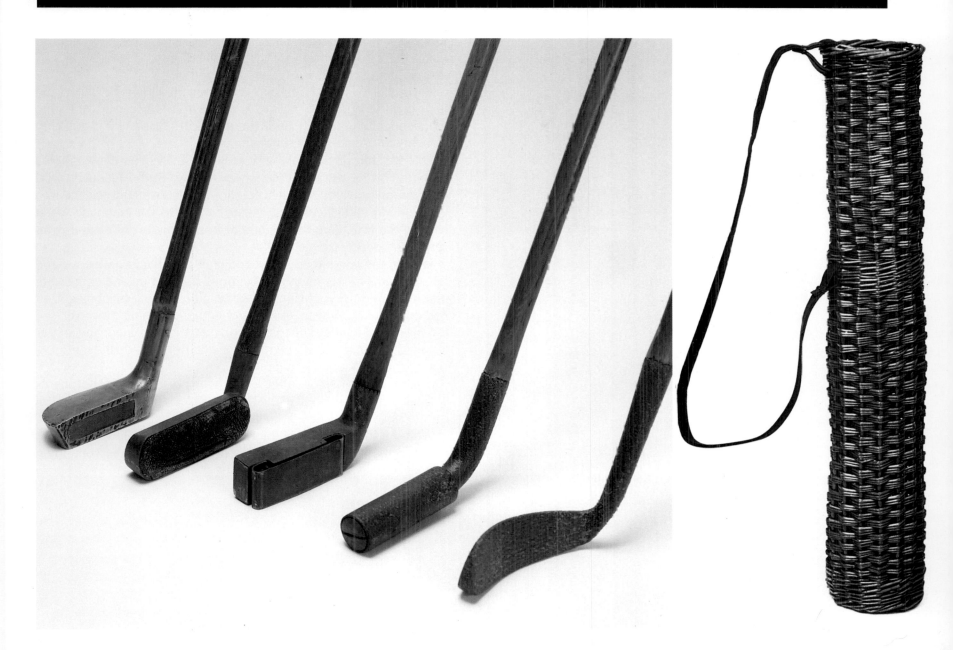

Experts soon noticed that towards the end of each round this problem seemed to cure itself and they realised that a slightly 'damaged' ball flew better than a new one. Consequently, artificial 'damage' marks were added to the gutties. And so was born the dimple.

Towards the end of the 19th century the life of the gutty in turn came to an end, because of American Coburn Haskell who invented the rubber-cored ball. His new invention wrapped an elastic thread around a rubber core and covered it in a plastic coating.

Not popular at first, Haskell's ball was used by Alex Herd in the 1902 British Open. He outdrove his fellow competitors and beat the great Harry Vardon and James Braid into joint second place. From then on the Haskell ball became widely used.

The modern-day golf ball had been born and since then has undergone minor changes. Perhaps surprisingly, it was not until 1920 that a standard weight for a golf ball was agreed by both the R&A and the US PGA. In 1921 the Americans launched their larger 1.68in (42.67mm) ball but British golfers stuck with their small ball of 1.62in (41.15mm). The use of the larger ball in the British Open has, however, been compulsory since 1974.

The improvement of the golf ball has made it possible for golfers not only to hit the ball further but to play controlled shots. But neither would have been possible on such a large scale had the improvement in the ball not coincided with similar advances in golf club manufacture.

The modern-day golfer has a choice of a maximum of 14 clubs in his golf bag. His forefathers rarely had more than two clubs to pick from and in many cases just one. Bags were unheard of and either the golfer or his caddy would carry the clubs under one arm.

As for graphite shafted clubs and the likes which the modern golfer utilises, well, they weren't even a dream of Harry Vardon or Tom Morris. Very early clubs were nothing more than a stick with a suitably shaped 'clubhead' with which to hit the ball. Because a golfer would often have just one club to his name, it would have to be an all-purpose one suitable for driving and putting. There is little

documented evidence of what golf clubs were made out of in the 15th, 16th or 17th centuries, but towards the end of the 18th century shafts are known to have been made of hazel or ash with a head made of beech, apple, pear or blackthorn. The two components would be glued together and the joints bound in twine. The club faces were often very narrow (approximately 1 in) and were usually 4-5 in long.

Although it is not known what the earliest clubs were made of, it is known that golfers soon realised the need to have different clubs for various shots and they soon developed clubs with varying lofts. The club used for good lies was what they called the 'play club'. It was the forerunner of the driver. The putter was also a wooden headed club, but was frequently used for approach shots to the green from good lies.

With the advent of the gutty there came a need to redesign the clubs because the new ball was putting a strain on the clubs at the junction of the head and shaft. Club heads were made shorter in an effort to lessen the blow caused by hitting the gutty. Soft woods were found to be more suitable for the heads but there was still a problem with the shafts. Ash was not suitable for the new ball but it was found that North American hickory was an ideal wood for golf club shafts.

Hickory was springy and was ideal for hitting the gutty with. This whippy quality was also responsible for a change in the golf swing of many of the players of the day. No longer was there the need merely to sweep the ball on its way, as was the case with the feathery. A more upright swing was adopted, and the club was allowed to do much of the work. The problem of shaft and head joints was resolved by inserting the shaft into a bored hole in the head.

Iron-headed clubs had by now become popular. Initially they were invented for getting the ball away from difficult lies but by now they were used as an aid to playing controlled approach shots. The leading professionals towards the end of the 19th century were such fine exponents with irons that manufacturers started standardising the shape of the club-head, which had previously been irregular in

shape and design, and such irons as the cleek (modern day equivalent is the 2 iron), jigger (4 iron), mashie (5 iron), mashie-niblick (7 iron) and niblick (8/9 iron) became popular.

Top golfers were now equipped with anything from 7-9 clubs (and their caddies now had bags to keep them in). Advances of equipment and technique had made this increase necessary. But golf club design was continuing to change.

With the introduction of the Haskell ball an even harder wood was required for the wooden clubheads and the North American wood persimmon provided the ideal solution. Inserts were also added into the wooden club faces to prevent damage to the clubhead when striking the ball. Originally made of bone or ivory, modern-day inserts are plastic.

Prior to the late 19th century, golf club manufacture was by hand but such was the demand that factories were set up and clubs were manufactured on sophisticated lathes and turning machines. Golf had come a long way in less than one hundred years. However, the top players of the day still insisted on their clubs being made and/or repaired by hand and such craftsmen survived despite the introduction of the club-making machine.

A shortage of hickory after World War I resulted in experiments with steel shafts and in 1926 the US Golf Association gave its approval for their use. The British followed in 1930.

With the introduction of the mass produced steel-shafted club it became possible to produce a 'matched set' of golf clubs; something

the golfer had not enjoyed the benefit of in the past. The named clubs of the past like niblick and mashie were long gone, and clubs were now known by numbers which, in a way, summed it all up. Gone was the craftsman who custom-made the hickory-shafted mashie-niblick. In his place came the machine which produced the 8 iron. But that is progress and despite the tragic demise of the talented club-maker, it made way for an improvement of equipment that was to bring an improvement in standards.

As golfers sought to bring more sophistication into their game in the 1930s club manufacturers tried to capitalise by producing a wide range of '½' clubs; 1½ iron, 2½ iron etc. Caddies were lugging bags around courses with over 20 clubs in. It was then that the USGA and R & A decided on the present-day limit of 14 clubs.

Persimmon eventually became in short supply and wooden-headed clubs were made out of a laminated material and today golfers use these 'woods' as well as 'woods' made with aluminum heads. And of course, the graphite shafts, while more expensive then steel, are more supple and can offer greater distance.

However, golf is about more than clubs and the golf ball. The accessories like golf bag, golf trolley, gloves, spiked shoes and tees help make the game so much easier than in those early days of championship golf little more than one hundred years ago. How good would Young Tom Morris have been with a graphite-shafted club and rubber-cored ball? How good would Jack Nicklaus have been with a hickory-shafted mashie-niblick and a gutty?

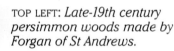

TOP LEFT: *Late-19th century persimmon woods made by Forgan of St Andrews.*

LEFT: *By the turn of the 20th century golf club manufacture had become a mass production operation as can be seen at Forgan's enlarged factory.*

TOP RIGHT: *An early set of steel shafted clubs c.1930.*

RIGHT: *. . . and after all those changes, this is what the modern-day golfers uses.*

THE WORLD'S GREAT COURSES

By the time golfers were playing with steel-shafted clubs and the rubber cored ball, most of the world's great golf courses had been established and were gaining a reputation for providing a true test of the ability of the top golfers who challenged them.

Naturally, Scotland can rightfully claim to have some of the finest golf courses in the world. We have already seen how St Andrews and Prestwick developed but what a wonderful selection of courses that country has to offer to championship golfer and casual player alike.

In the early days of the British Open, St Andrews and Prestwick shared the staging of the championship with **Musselburgh**, the then home of the Honourable Company of Edinburgh Golfers. Situated at Prestonpans in East Lothian, it is believed to have been established in 1760 although evidence confirms that it was certainly in existence in 1774.

The original course measured seven holes and an eighth was added in 1833. The course was shared by the Honourable Company, the Bruntsfield Links and the Royal Burgess Society. It attained its 'Royal' status in 1876 when the Duke of Connaught became the club's president. Musselburgh staged its first British Open in 1874 when Mungo Park won by two strokes from Young Tom Morris. it was used five more times but was taken off the rota in 1891 when the Honourable Company took their headquarters to Muirfield.

Musselburgh may no longer be a major championship course, but it certainly stakes a claim as part of golfing heritage. Not only did it play a significant role in the early days of the Open but it is also the home of the oldest golf competition in the world and in 1810 was the home of the first ever women's golf tournament.

After the Honourable Company of Edinburgh Golfers left Musselburgh they established their new home at **Muirfield**. And because they were one of the three co-organisers of the British Open, the championship was held at Muirfield for the first time in 1892, the year after the Honourable Company took up tenure. Royal Liverpool's Harold Hilton was Muirfield's first champion.

Like Musselburgh, Muirfield is situated in East Lothian on the shores of the Firth of Forth and is a true championship course that is much respected by the world's top golfers. One of the biggest hazards at Muirfield is the wind.

In its early days, aficionados took great pride in denigrating Muirfield as a suitable venue for the Open. This was largely due to the Honourable Company's decision to move their headquarters and thus deprive golf of what had been one of its great championship courses, Musselburgh. But after undergoing some changes, notably to make it look more like a links course, Muirfield soon gained popularity, particularly with spectators, because it is an excellent viewing course.

Muirfield has seen some memorable moments in Open history including Henry Cotton's great round of 66 in the 1948 championship which was witnessed by King George VI. Jack Nicklaus conquered all, including the rough, to win the Open at Muirfield in 1966, and in 1980 Japan's Isao Aoki had a British Open record equalling 63. But it is not just the Open that has been held at Muirfield. It has also played host to the leading amateur tournaments including the Walker Cup, and in 1973 was the first Scottish course to stage the Ryder Cup. After St Andrews it is the most senior of all current British Open venues.

Scotland has had three other British Open courses, all of which have proved to be popular venues over the years.

Troon was first used in 1923 and is still on the Championship rota today. Situated north of Ayr, its undulating fairways and severe rough make it a real test of any championship golfer. The winds coming in off the Firth of Clyde are so strong at times that fish are reported to have been blown on to greens at Troon. The club was founded in 1878 and the first Open was won by Arthur Havers. But one of Troon's favorite 'sons' is Arnold Palmer who won his second Open title there by a staggering six strokes in 1962 from Kel Nagle. This was also Jack Nicklaus' first Open appearance but he only just made the cut after a first round 80 including a 10 at the 11th.

Troon's 577-yard 6th hole is one of the longest in championship golf while the 8th, known as the Postage Stamp, is one of the shortest ever used for the British Open. But what nostalgia there was at that hole in the 1973 Open when 71-year-old Gene Sarazen holed in one in front of the TV cameras.

Troon has been used for the Open on six occasions and one behind is another of Scotland's great courses, **Carnoustie**. First

OPPOSITE PAGE: *Alexander (Alister) McKenzie (right) was one of the world's finest golf course architects and was responsible for such fine courses as Augusta*

National, Royal Melbourne and Cypress Point.

ABOVE: *The short 16th at Gleneagles' King's Course.*

used for the Open in 1931 when American Tommy Armour lifted the title, it has not been used since 1975, when Tom Watson won the first of his five Opens. Carnoustie is one of the longest courses in Britain and its 7252 yards for the 1968 British Open made it the longest in Open history. Built on public ground at Angus, it was founded in 1842. Its closing three holes are certainly the most daunting in championship golf.

The final Scottish course to have been used for the British Open is **Turnberry**, first used in 1977, and again in 1986. The Turnberry Hotel Golf Club was founded in 1903 and overlooks the Isle of Arran and Ailsa Craig rock. There are two courses at Turnberry, the championship Ailsa Course and the Arran course.

Only two World Wars prevented Turnberry from gaining earlier selection as a venue for the British Open. During both hostilities the site was used as an airfield and during World War II the course was extensively damaged by airfield construction work. It was only due to the remarkable skills of Mackenzie Ross that the Ailsa course was re-paired before re-opening in 1951.

By the time it was chosen for the 1977 Open it had been used for a variety of major championships including the Walker Cup. When it made its Open debut in 1977 it was felt by many to be too easy, as Tom Watson and Jack Nicklaus destroyed all opposition, and the course, with a barrage of British Open records. When Greg Norman won at Turnberry in 1986 it was certainly more severe.

Not all Scotland's great courses have staged the Open. The King's Course at **Gleneagles**, for example, is one of the finest courses north of the border, but partly because it is not a links course, it has never staged the great championship. Situated at Auchterarder in

Perthshire and overlooking the Grampians and Ochils, its setting is one of the finest of all British golf courses.

There are in fact four courses in the Gleneagles complex at the moment and the King's and Queen's, the most testing of these, have been in existence since 1919 while the famous Gleneagles Hotel opened in 1924. The original two courses were designed by James Braid.

Although it has never staged the British Open, Gleneagles has played host to most great championships and in 1921 was the venue for the first match between the professionals of the United States and Great Britain, which was the forerunner of the Ryder Cup.

Not all great British courses are in Scotland, England has its fair share of great courses and among the finest is **Wentworth** at Virginia Water, Surrey. The Wentworth Club opened as recently as 1924 with first the East Course and then the West Course. It is the latter which became the more frequently used of the two in championship play. Because of its length of approximately 7000 yards it is known affectionately as 'The Burma Road'. The par 5 17th is one of the great par 5s in championship golf. Wentworth is the home of the World Match-Play Championship each year and has also staged the Ryder Cup, Canada Cup, and Curtis Cup, among others.

One of England's great modern-day championship courses is **Royal Birkdale** which is one of the many fine links courses along the Fylde coast between Freshfield and Southport, Lancashire. Although founded by local enthusiasts in 1889 at a site nearer to the town center than its present home, the course moved to its new, and current, home in 1897. The course was redesigned in 1931 and the clubhouse is one of the finest in Britain.

Birkdale was granted 'Royal' patronage in 1951 and three years later staged its first British Open when Australian Peter Thomson won the first of two Opens over the famous links. Although it has staged championship golf since 1909 it is only since the war years that the testing course has been used for major international cham-

ABOVE: *The 15th fairway and green at Royal Birkdale.*

RIGHT: *The 8th at Turnberry's Ailsa course. The Arran hills make a wonderful backdrop to this beautiful course.*

pionships and has since been the home of the Walker Cup, Ryder Cup, and Curtis Cup. There is a special plaque at Birkdale's 16th hole to commemorate a brilliant shot played by Arnold Palmer during the 1961 British Open.

Another course to erect a plaque as a reminder of a great Palmer achievement can be found at **Cherry Hills**, just one of the dozens of world-famous American courses. The Cherry Hills plaque was erected as a reminder of how Palmer made up a seven stroke deficit on leader Mike Souchak in the final round of the 1960 US Open to win the title for the one and only time.

Cherry Hills is situated about one mile above sea level in Denver, Colorado. A feature of many US golf holes is the creek running alongside the fairway. The 14th dog-leg par 4 at Cherry Hills is one of the finest. Cherry Hills has been used for the US Open three times, the first in 1938 and the last to date in 1978 when Andy North won the title.

The United States has so many outstanding golf courses. There are Winged Foot, Pebble Beach, Shinnecock Hills, Baltusrol, the PGA National, Oakland Hills, Pinehurst and many, many, more. But for probably the most beautiful golf course in the world you have to look no further than **Augusta National** in Georgia, the home of the Masters since its inauguration in 1934.

The Masters and the Augusta National were the brainchild of Atlanta-born Bobby Jones, the finest amateur golfer the world has ever seen. Jones, and his friend Clifford Roberts, came up with the idea of both course and tournament and it was after recruiting the services of top designer Alister Mackenzie that their dreams were fulfilled when it was completed in 1931. (Mackenzie was also responsible for the design of another of America's top courses, Cypress Point.) The club was named the Augusta National because it was Jones' intention that members should be drawn from all over the United States, not just from Atlanta.

Each hole at Augusta is named after the flower or shrub which borders it. For example, the 1st is Tea Olive, the 2nd Pink Dogwood, 3rd Flowering Peach, and so on. The very fast greens and an abundance of water makes Augusta a course that can only be beaten by the very best of players, like Jack Nicklaus, who has won the Masters a record six times. Anything but the very best of golf at Augusta is fatal. The course is continually waiting to punish those wayward shots.

The United States also possesses the course which was voted the best golf course in the world by a panel of golfers and golf experts in *Golf* magazine in September 1989.

Pine Valley is one of golf's most spectacular courses and the second hole is one of the truly great golf holes. A short par 4, its fairway is littered with bunkers. Standing on the tee and looking to the green some 350 yards away it is a spectacular sight and the temptation is to take out a camera rather than a driver.

Every hole at Pine Valley has its own very distinctive features which add to the overall beauty of the course.

Situated at Clementon, New Jersey, the course was developed by George Crump, the owner of the Colonnades Hotel in Philadelphia. He dug out the previously untouched forest area of New Jersey and took advantage of the natural sandy soil. He was aided in his design by the British architect H S Colt and between them they developed an outstanding course. The first 14 holes were opened in 1916 and since that day it has been widely regarded as the most difficult golf course in the world. Only the finest of tee shots are good enough to steer clear of the woods and sand which abound around the fairways. Many golfers have walked off the course in despair.

Pebble Beach is one of the most beautiful, spectacular and exciting golf courses in the world; its 7th hole is one of the most photographed holes in golf. It is just over 100 yards in length but the green juts out into the Pacific Ocean to give a spectacular setting. But there are other dramatic holes at Pebble Beach. The second shot at the 8th requires a carry over a 100ft drop into the ocean, and the 18th, along the rocky coastline, is perhaps one of the finest finishing holes in championship golf.

Pebble Beach is on the Monterey peninsula, approximately 120 miles south of San Francisco, and was the first of several fine courses

OPPOSITE PAGE: *Just one of the many spectacular golf holes to be found in the United States. This one is at Illinois' Kempler Lakes Club, home of the 1989 PGA Championship.*

ABOVE: *They don't put trees on golf courses for beauty's sake . . . as Lee Trevino is finding out here, during the 1984 PGA Championship.*

to be developed in the area. Cypress Point, Monterey and Spyglass Hill followed later. Pebble Beach was built in 1918 and its par 72 now measures 6799 yards.

Sharing the Monterey peninsular with Pebble Beach is **Cypress Point**; widely regarded as the most beautiful golf course in the world. Laid out in the 1920s it is not a long course but is certainly a testing one. Because of its length it has not been used for major championship golf.

The variety of fairways and greens add to its overall beauty and the short 16th, like Pebble Beach's 7th, is one of the great golf holes for the photographer. It is also one of golf's great disaster holes. It is so severe it has led to Cypress Point being described as; 'the best 17 hole golf course in the world.' The tee shot, depending on the tee in use, may require as much as a 200-yard carry across the Pacific to a green situated on an island high above the ocean.

ABOVE: *Wentworth in Surrey is one of England's finest courses and is the home of the World Match-Play Championship each year. The photo shows Nick Faldo in action in the 1989 tournament.*

RIGHT: *Royal Troon, just one of Scotland's many British Open courses. It played host to the 1989 Open but Australian Greg Norman will wish to forget this shot; he played out of bounds from the bunker during the play-off.*

LEFT: *The famous Hogan's Bridge at the Augusta National course, home of the Masters. 1988 winner Sandy Lyle is shown.*

Of course, not all the world's best golf courses are confined to Britain and the United States. One of the finest outside those two countries is the **Royal Melbourne** course in Australia.

The oldest club with continuous membership in Australia, it was opened in July 1891 thanks to the efforts of William Knox and J M Bruce. The official uniform for members at the time was a scarlet coat with gold buttons, knickerbockers and Tam O'Shanter. A new course was laid out in the Sandringham district of Melbourne in 1901 and its deep bunkers helped make it a true championship course and one of the finest inland courses in the world. This course was later re-named the West Course after the construction of a new East course in 1932. The leading course designer Dr Alister Mackenzie

was brought from Britain to suggest major alterations to the original course and assist with the design of the new course.

For major championships a composite course using holes from the West and East can be created to make a real test of the professional golfer's ability.

Melbourne, like St Andrews, Pine Valley, Augusta, and every golf course in the world, has one thing in common . . . it is unique. Whether a golf course be in the United States, or in Australia, France, Sweden, Japan or Scotland, there will never be another course like it. Each golf course has its own peculiarities, its own temptations, and its own beauty. Those qualities all go towards making this great game so attractive.

THE PROFESSIONALS' RISE IN STATURE

At the time of Francis Ouimet's surprise win in the 1913 US Open, professional golfers in both America and Britain may well have had some of the finest golf courses in the world on which to play but they still had a major obstacle to overcome; their poor standing in the eyes of golf's administrators.

Particularly in America there was 'hostility' towards the tournament professionals who were often treated virtually as lepers. They were not allowed to use club houses and the other facilities that were readily available to amateur members. Such was the 'class' distinction that amateur winners of major tournaments were prefixed with the word 'Mr' whereas professional winners were, for some unknown reason, not 'Misters' although they belonged to the same race and were the same sex as their amateur counterparts.

The problem had been eased in Britain with the formation of the Professional Golfers' Association in 1901 thanks largely to the efforts of one of the leading professionals of the day, J H Taylor. He felt the need for an association because he could see that professional golfers were being exploited. But in America they still had to overcome that 'unwanted' feeling.

In the same year that Ouimet captured American hearts, the leading British professionals Harry Vardon and Ted Ray embarked upon a tour of the United States to help popularize the game. They certainly did that and played to 'full houses' wherever they went. By the time they arrived at Brookline in September they were the two clear favorites to lift the US Open crown but then the frail looking Ouimet stepped in and upset their plans.

Three years after Ouimet's triumph, the Professional Golfers' Association of America was founded in New York. It was styled on its British counterpart and used the British PGA's constitution as the basis for its own. The US PGA was formed thanks to the efforts of businessmen and amateur golfers, notably Rodman Wanamaker of Philadelphia. But the man who did most to improve the professionals' lot was the flamboyant Walter Hagen.

Ouimet was the man who suddenly made golf front page news in the United States, but it was Hagen who took the game to the ordinary people. His contribution to golf's rise in popularity was immense and his role in getting better conditions for the professional golfer must never be forgotten by professionals the world over. A great innovator, Hagen was as well known for his extrovert nature, both on

BELOW: *Gene Sarazen was one of the leading professionals in the 1920s and 30s. He is pictured here with his wife on the way to play in England in 1924.*

RIGHT: *Walter Hagen (with cigarette in hand) shakes hands with Aubrey Boomer before a match. Arnaud Massy, 1907 British Open winner, looks on.*

ABOVE: *Walter Hagen being watched by his 1933 Ryder Cup team-mates. They, and other golf professionals at that time, owed Hagen a big debt because of his role in getting better facilities and recognition for the professional golfer.*

and off the golf course, as he was for his outstanding golfing skills. He gave golf the plus-fours. And he also gave his fellow professionals the right to hold their heads high for the first time in the United States.

Hagen broke down that barrier between the stiff-upper-lipped committees and the professionals at golf clubs on both sides of the Atlantic and no longer did professionals have to use side entrances when they entered clubs. At last he gained access to changing rooms and the catering facilities offered by leading clubs in the United States and Britain. It was a major breakthrough.

The 'Haig' was a great crowd puller. Consequently, clubs had little alternative but to welcome him and his fellow professionals with open arms. The barrier had been broken and the way was open for professionals to make a real impact on the world of golf. And that impact has not waned since the days of Walter Hagen.

Coincidentally Hagen had finished in joint fourth place behind Ouimet in the 1913 US Open. Ouimet was, of course, an amateur, but the first one to take advantage of his miraculous 'door-opening' performance was Hagen who won the Open in 1914 and 1919. He was also a master at match-play golf and won the US PGA Championship (then a match-play tournament) five times in seven years between 1921-27. He also delighted the British crowds and captured the

British Open four times between 1922-29. He was the first of the great post-World War I tournament professionals. At Troon in 1923 he was involved in a typical Hagen incident. Runner-up in the Open to Arthur Havers, Hagen refused to enter the clubhouse for the presentation because professionals had been refused admission all week. Instead, he invited the waiting fans over the road to a nearby pub where Hagen conducted his own celebrations.

He had the ability to mix with people at all levels and once got the Prince of Wales (later King Edward VII) to hold the flag for him while he was making a putt. The King to be was affectionately known as 'Eddie' to Hagen. How could somebody with connections like that not be allowed into the changing room of a golf club?

By the mid twenties America had produced some fine tournament professionals although Jerome Travers and Charles Evans kept striking the odd blow for the amateur golfer. The likes of Jim Barnes and Gene Sarazen, along with Hagen, were dominant on each side of the Atlantic. Resorts, hotels, and Chambers of Commerce, realized the publicity and commercial value of professional golf coming to town and they were much sought after personalities. The professional golfer was here to stay and they demanded and got the rights and facilities they deserved.

But despite their great skill and new found admiration in the world of golf, the professionals had to take a back seat in the second half of the 1920s to a young amateur golfer from Georgia. His name? Robert Tyre Jones.

AN AMATEUR WHO STOLE THE GLORY

Hagen and Sarazen may well have been the outstanding professionals in the 1920s but even the extrovert Hagen was upstaged by an amateur from Georgia, Robert Tyre Jones, known simply as Bob or Bobby.

Jones is widely regarded as the finest golfer of all time, a claim that was certainly uncontested until the arrival of Jack Nicklaus. There are still many who believe Jones to be the most complete golfer ever, yet he never turned professional throughout his all-too-short career.

Born in Atlanta in 1902, Jones graduated from college with degrees in law, literature and engineering, and it was to the first of these that he would turn for his future as he became a Georgia lawyer. Jones resisted many lucrative offers to turn professional and carried on with his legal practice. But in between he made a name for himself in the world of golf.

Having started playing golf at the age of five Jones soon realised the importance of a good swing. He developed one of the finest which took him to the top during his brief career.

He made his US Amateur debut in 1916 at the age of 14, and four years later appeared in his first US Open. Three years later, in 1923, he won the title for the first time when he beat Bobby Cruickshank in a play-off at Inwood. That was to herald the start of a remarkable run of success which saw Jones win 13 amateur and professional majors. In addition he appeared in the first US Walker Cup team of 1922 and appeared in every one up to the time of his retirement in 1930.

The year after winning the US Open he captured the first of five US Amateur titles when he beat George Von Elm 9 & 8 in the final at Merion. He retained his title at Oakmont in 1925 and a year later had the distinction of winning the Open championships of both Great Britain and the United States.

At Royal Lytham he beat a host of American professionals like Al Watrous, Walter Hagen and George Von Elm who were all left trailing behind Jones who had four consistent rounds of 72, 72, 73, and 74 to win by two strokes. When he won the US title at Scioto he won by one shot from Joe Turnesa despite returning a 79 in the 2nd round. It was another 'double' in 1927. This time he paired a six stroke win in the British Open at St Andrews with his third US Amateur title when he beat Chick Evans 8 & 7 at Minikahda, Minnesota.

Compared to his recent run of success 1928 could well be described as a 'bad' year for Jones. He won only one title, the US Amateur at Brae Burn, Massachussetts, but again it was another easy win as this time he beat the British champion Phil Perkins 10 & 9 in the final. Jones appeared in his fourth Walker Cup match in 1928 and had the honor of captaining the side for the first time. Needless to say the United States won, 11-1, and Jones remained undefeated. In his singles he inflicted another big defeat upon Perkins, this time by 13 & 12.

The following year Jones won the US Open for the third time when he beat Al Espinosa in a play-off at Winged Foot. Jones carded two 7s in his final round and then had to sink a 12-foot putt at the last to tie with Espinosa. The play-off however, was a very one sided affair with Jones winning by 23 strokes over 36 holes. Victory for Jones made up for his one stroke defeat by Johnny Farrell in a play-off the previous year at Olympia Fields.

By the end of 1929 Jones had won the US Open three times, the British Open twice, the US Amateur four times and appeared on four Walker Cup teams. However he had never won the British Amateur title. Twelve months later he was to increase each of those totals by one as he completed the greatest achievement ever known in the history of golf when he won all those four major tournaments in one year, and also skippered the winning Walker Cup team.

His remarkable year started on 31 May when he beat Britain's Roger Wethered 7 & 5 to win the British Amateur title at St Andrews. Less than a month later he won the British Open at Hoylake when he beat American professionals Leo Diegel and Macdonald Smith by two strokes. When Jones won the US Open at Interlachen, Mac-

ABOVE: *Bobby Jones wooed them of all ages and sexes when he appeared at St Andrews for the British Open in 1927. He went on to retain his title by a six stroke margin from Aubrey Boomer, Fred Robson and many other top professionals of the day. Jones resisted all temptations to turn professional throughout his all-too-short career.*

donald Smith was again two strokes behind in second place. Jones had now won three legs of an 'impossible' Grand Slam. Even if he didn't win the final leg, the first three were enough to put him into the records books, and earn him the accolade of 'greatest Golfer of all time.' But he did achieve success in that final leg.

On 27 September 1930, fans by the thousands flocked to Merion to witness the completion of the finest golfing achievement ever seen, as Jones completed an easy 8 & 7 victory over Eugene Homans to clinch the US Amateur title. It was over the same course that Jones won his first amateur title six years earlier.

Bobby Jones was only 28 at the time of the Grand Slam and he confirmed rumors that he was about to retire from competitive golf to concentrate on his legal business. Despite many tempting offers to come out of retirement Jones stuck to his word but that was not the end of his association with the game that had given him so much pleasure.

He made a series of instructional films because he wanted to give back to golf what he had taken out of it. He was also largely instrumental in the foundation of the Augusta National Golf Course and the US Masters which is played over that beautiful course every year. Both serve as a memorial to the game's finest golfer.

Suffering from a severe spinal disease from 1950, Jones still made the journey to St Andrews in 1958 for the inaugural Eisenhower Trophy match. At the same time the people of St Andrews bestowed the Freedom of the Burgh upon him in recognition of his triumphs 28 years earlier.

Sadly Jones became paralysed in his arms and legs and he died at Augusta in 1971 at the age of 69. A true golfing legend was gone.

ABOVE LEFT: *There was no keeping the fans away from Interlachen in 1930; they all wanted to see Bob Jones complete the third leg of his amazing Grand Slam.*

ABOVE: *Jones stands proudly with his four trophies after completing his 1930 Grand Slam. From left to right they are: British Open, US Amateur, British Amateur, US Open.*

RIGHT: *Bob Jones (left) receives the Freedom of the Burgh of St Andrews from the Provost, R Leonard, in 1958. Jones came to St Andrews for the inaugural Eisenhower Trophy.*

LEFT: *The nearest Al Watrous came to winning a 'Major' was at Royal Lytham in 1926 but Bobby Jones beat him by two strokes to win the Open.*

TEAM COMPETITIONS TO THE FORE

The first major team competition to arrive in the world of golf was the Walker Cup; initially an annual match between amateur players from Britain and the United States. But why the British should want to be involved in the start of such a match while the dominant Bobby Jones was around is hard to comprehend. Nevertheless, they were, and furthermore they wanted to show the world that British amateurs were as good as their American cousins. But it was not until eight years after Jones' retirement that they eventually got their name engraved on the famous trophy.

The idea of an international tournament, not just between Britain and the United States, was mooted by Herbert Walker, the President of the US Golf Association, who had visited St Andrews in 1920 to discuss the rules of golf with the R & A. He had discussed plans with his British counterparts about organising a challenge match and his fellow USGA members gave their approval and said they would donate a trophy, to be called the International Challenge Trophy. However, it was the media who renamed it the Walker Cup, and that name has stuck.

The USGA invited several countries to send teams to play for the Walker Cup in 1921. None responded to the invitation. Undaunted, however, the USGA assembled a makeshift team under the leadership of William C Fownes. They travelled to Hoylake to play a British team the day before the British Amateur Championship. The Americans won by nine matches to three in what was the first unofficial Walker Cup match. Playing for Britain that day was Tommy Armour. Five years later he played for America against Britain in the forerunner of the Ryder Cup.

However, the first official Walker Cup match came a year later when the R & A sent a team to America to challenge for the Cup at the National Golf Links of America in New York. Since then all Walker Cup matches have been between the United States and Great Britain and Ireland.

The first official match saw the Americans win by eight matches to four. One of Britain's victors was that well known golfing writer and journalist Bernard Darwin who was covering the event for *The Times* of London. He was called in to replace the Great Britain skipper Robert Harris who became ill and Darwin did his country proud by beating William C Fownes 3 & 1 in their singles match. Great Britain fared slightly better in the return at St Andrews a year later. This time they lost by just one match, 6-5. Since then the Walker Cup has been held every two years, with the venue alternating between Britain and the United States. But the superiority has remained with the Americans.

By the end of the first decade of Walker Cup golf, big victories for the American team were commonplace and after Bobby Jones' retirement in 1930 the US team was skippered by Francis Ouimet, who, appropriately, made his debut as captain in 1932 at Brookline where he had had his famous US Open victory.

Ouimet skippered the side six times and was only once on the losing side; that was on the occasion of Great Britain's first win in 1938 which was also to be their last win until 1971 when current R & A secretary Michael Bonallack led the side to a memorable success at St Andrews. Sadly there has been little for British fans to cheer since then as the American's have proved for more than sixty years that their amateur golfers are superior to their British counterparts. However, in 1989 the British Amateurs did something their Ryder Cup counterparts did in 1987 and won the Cup on US soil for the first time.

ABOVE LEFT: *The Great Britain team which took part in the first match against the United States in 1921. It was the forerunner of the Walker Cup. Back left is Tommy Armour who later played in the Ryder Cup for the USA.*

LEFT: *The US team from 1921. Second from the right at the front is Bobby Jones, and back left is Francis Ouimet.*

RIGHT: *The Walker Cup.*

LEFT: *The 1926 US Walker Cup team. They won the match 6½-5½, with the most notable individual victory being Bobby Jones' 12 and 11 win over Cyril Tolley.*

RIGHT: *Walker Cup action 1930: The large crowd at Sandwich's 6th green have a good vantage point to watch the foursomes match between Jones and Willing (USA) and Torrance and Hartley (GB). The American pair won 8 & 7.*

LEFT: *Bobby Jones (right) shakes hands with the Great Britain captain Roger Wethered before the 1930 Walker Cup match. It was Jones' last appearance in the competition.*

The British women have enjoyed marginally more success than their male counterparts in their biennial contest with the Americans in the Curtis Cup, but not a lot.

Although the Curtis Cup was founded in 1932, an international match between women golfers from Britain and the United States was held at Cromer, England, in 1905. It was the first ever match between the two countries, and the British ladies won 6-1. In the American side that day were the sisters Harriot and Margaret Curtis, and it was at their suggestion that the biennial competition was started in 1932. The USGA did the organising and financing on behalf of the American ladies while the Ladies' Golf Union did so for the British women.

The first match was played at Wentworth and it went the way of so many others with the Americans winning. Britain's captain was Joyce Wethered and the winning team was skippered by Marion Hollins. It was another American victory in the first match on US soil, at the Chevy Chase Club, Maryland, in 1934, but at Gleneagles two years later the British girls showed great spirit to earn a tie thanks to Jessie Anderson who holed a 20-foot putt on the last green to win her match and tie the contest.

The British girls had a good run in the 1950s when they won at Muirfield in 1952, at Prince's in 1956, and forced a tie at Massachusetts in 1958. But there wasn't any glory for the British again until 1986 when they had a great 13-5 win at Prairie Dunes, Kansas, to register only their third win. But more significantly, it was their first on US soil. Two games later the British girls had their first home win for 32 years.

Since the formation of the Walker and Curtis Cup competitions, other team competitions have been launched.

The Canada Cup, now the World Cup, for two-man teams from world-wide golfing nations was launched in 1953. America has also dominated that competition, just as they have done with the World Amateur Team Championship (for the Eisenhower Trophy) which was launched in 1958. The Eisenhower Trophy is for four man teams and was similar to the idea George Herbert Walker had back in 1920.

A women's world amateur team championship was launched in 1964. They contest the Espirito Santo Trophy every two years and, would you believe, it has been dominated by the American girls.

Since then the other two major international team tournaments to have been launched are the Kirin Cup and Dunhill Cup, both for male professionals.

The Kirin Cup World Championship of Golf was launched in 1985 when sponsored by Nissan. It is a team tournament for teams representing the world's leading golfing tours; US PGA Tour, Japan PGA Tour, European PGA Tour, and Australia/New Zealand PGA Tour. Surprise, surprise! The US PGA Tour has won three of the four tournaments up to 1988.

The Dunhill Cup, played at St Andrews, Scotland, is for three-man teams of professionals. It was launched in 1985 and the first four winners were: Australia, Australia, England, Ireland ... what! no America? Oh well, it just goes to show you can't win 'em all.

But the one team tournament in which the Americans have done a lot of winning over the years is the most prestigious of all team competitions in the world of golf, the Ryder Cup.

SAM RYDER'S TOURNAMENT

Although their hold on the cup has been a bit wobbly in recent years, the professional golfers from America have had a firm grip on the Ryder Cup just as they have most other team tournaments.

The best known team tournament in golf, the Ryder Cup was the brainchild of English seed merchant Samuel Ryder. Hailing from the north of England, he left his father's market garden business at Sale, Cheshire, before the turn of the century to set up his own business in St Albans, Hertfordshire. At his new home he became a respected member of the local community and served the town as a councillor, justice of the peace, church deacon and mayor. But over-work brought about ill-health and it was on the suggestion of a local Church Minister, Reverend Frank Wheeler, that Ryder took up golf as

a form of relaxation. He joined the Verulam Club in St Albans and golf suddenly became the new 'love' of his life.

He became as involved with the sport as he had with his business and other interests and was three times appointed captain of the club. He became a great friend of many of the day's top professionals and readily made cash available to bring the top stars to the Verulam club to compete in tournaments. Among his best friends were the Triumvirate of Taylor, Braid and Vardon. Another good friend of Ryder's was local professional Abe Mitchell. And, probably at the suggestion of Mitchell, Ryder put up a cup to be contested by professional golfers from Britain and the United States. The figure on the lid of the Ryder Cup trophy is modelled on Mitchell.

ABOVE: *The Great Britain team which made the trip to Worcester, Massachusetts, for the first Ryder Cup match in 1927.*

RIGHT: *Aubrey Boomer was one of the last survivors from the inaugural Ryder Cup match. Sadly he died in 1989.*

LEFT: *Huge galleries flocked to Gleneagles in 1921 to see the first match between professionals from Great Britain and the United States. It was the forerunner of the Ryder Cup which was instituted six years later.*

ABOVE: *Gene Sarazen was a stalwart of the US Ryder Cup team in its early days and did not miss a match until 1947.*

ABOVE RIGHT: *The very distinctive putting style of Leo Diegel. He had a great Ryder Cup debut in 1927, beating the Great Britain captain Ted Ray 7 & 5 in the singles.*

LEFT: *Charles Whitcombe captained the Great Britain Ryder Cup team on four occasions, in 1931, 1935, 1937 and 1949. Only Dai Rees has skippered the side on more occasions. He is seen here during the 1927 Open at St Andrews when he was sixth.*

The inspiration for such a competition, to be contested biennially, came after the two nations met in a match at Wentworth in 1926, which Britain won 13½-1½. But when it got down to serious business a year later at Worcester, Massachusetts, the scoreline was reversed as the American won 9½-2½ under the leadership of Walter Hagen. The Great Britain side was led by Ted Ray.

Each team consisted of just eight men per side and play was completed over two days; 3-4 June 1927. This is how the scores in that historic first match read:

Foursomes

Walter Hagen/Johnny Golden (US) beat **Ted Ray/Fred Robson** 2 & 1

Johnny Farrell/Jim Turnesa (US) beat **George Duncan/Archie Compston** 8 & 6

Gene Sarazen/Al Watrous (US) beat **Arthur Havers/Herbert Jolly** 3 & 2

Aubrey Boomer/Charles Whitcombe (GB) beat **Leo Diegel/Bill Mehlhorn** 7 & 5

Singles

Bill Mehlhorn (US) beat **Archie Compston** 1 hole

Johnny Farrell (US) beat **Aubrey Boomer** 5 & 4

Johnny Golden (US) beat **Herbert Jolly** 8 & 7

Leo Diegel (US) beat **Ted Ray** 7 & 5

Gene Sarazen (US) and **Charles Whitcombe** halved

Walter Hagen (US) beat **Archie Havers** 2 & 1

Al Watrous (US) beat **Fred Robson** 3 & 2

George Duncan (GB) beat **Jim Turnesa** 1 hole

The British gained revenge two years later at Moortown, Leeds with a 7-5 win despite losing the foursomes. The outstanding match in the singles was that between the two captains, George Duncan and Walter Hagen. The British captain won that particular battle with a remarkable 10 & 8 scoreline.

Superiority swung back to the Americans at Scioto in 1931 with a comfortable 9-3 win. The US skipper Hagen made no mistakes in his singles this time when he beat the new British captain, Charles Whitcombe, 4 & 3

The seaside links of the Southport and Ainsdale Club was the setting for the 1933 Ryder Cup. Great Britain was skippered by J H Taylor in a non-playing capacity, and the Americans were again led by Hagen. Crowds never before seen at Ryder Cup matches flocked to the course, notably on the second day when they sensed a British victory.

Having won the foursomes for the first time the British lads went

ABOVE: *The man who started it all, Samuel Ryder (center) with the 1933 captains, Walter Hagen (right) and J H Taylor.*

BELOW: *Sam Snead (left) and Horton Smith dressed in the team blazers during the 1937 Ryder Cup. For Snead it was his Cup debut.*

RIGHT: *The large gallery at Southport & Ainsdale encouraged the home team to a narrow one point victory in the 1933 Ryder Cup. It turned out to be their last success for 24 years. Alf Padgham is shown driving at the 17th.*

into the second day leading by one point but as results were posted throughout day two, the lead kept changing and suddenly it came down to the match between Britain's Syd Easterbrook and Densmore Shute.

They came to the last all square. Easterbrook putted up for a guaranteed four. Shute putted past the hole and then surprisingly missed the return. Easterbrook won by one and assured Britain of the 1933 Ryder Cup but Easterbrook's moment of glory was to be the last enjoyed by the British team for 24 years. Shute and the Americans were to gain substantial compensation in the British Open shortly after. Shute beat Craig Wood in a play-off and Easterbrook was the only Briton in the top six.

Big wins by the Americans followed, no matter which side of the Atlantic they played, and despite the recruiting of such men as Henry Cotton, Dai Rees, Max Faulkner, Fred Daly and so on, the British team could not halt the run of American success and by the time the 1957 tournament came around, the United States held a 9-2 lead in the series.

Dai Rees had the honor of captaining the Great Britain side for a second time in 1957 and Jack Burke was debuting as the US captain. The match, held on 4-5 October was played over the Lindrick Course, near Sheffield. At the end of the foursomes an all-too-common

scoreline saw the Americans leading 3-1 and another win looked imminent. But how inspired the British boys were on day two as they won match after match in the singles. They won six of the eight singles, and halved one. Only Peter Alliss lost for the British team. It was the first time since 1933 that no American had won twice as Rees led his team to a memorable 7½-4½ victory.

Confidence was sky high for the return match at the Eldorado Country Club two years later. But how unfounded that proved to be as the Americans got back on the winning trail by a margin of 8½ matches to 2½.

The following years saw changes in the format. All matches, previously played over 36 holes, were reduced to 18 holes, but the number of foursomes matches was increased from four to eight, and singles matches from eight to 16. But changes in format did nothing to help the British team and it was not until after the recruitment of European players in 1979, and a change of name to *Europe*, that the Americans came under pressure for the first time since 1957.

The Americans had the Ryder Cup all their own way for far too long. Tony Jacklin and his band of men were ready to put the records straight and the 1980s has certainly belonged to the Europeans in terms of Ryder Cup glory as we will see later.

LEFT: *'Arnie's Army' even includes dogs! A stalwart of six Ryder Cups, Palmer was honored with the captaincy of the US team in 1963.*

RIGHT: *A delighted American team hoist their skipper Jack Burke into the air after retaining the Cup at Muirfield in 1973. Lee Trevino supports his right foot and Billy Casper his left.*

BELOW: *'Well played partner'. Maurice Bembridge (right) shakes the hand of his team-mate Brian Huggett after the pair had just beaten the top American duo of Nicklaus and Palmer in their fourball at Muirfield in 1973.*

THE BIRTH OF THE MASTERS

The world's first great championship, the British Open, was born in 1860. The US Open followed in 1895, the US PGA championship was first seen in 1916, and in 1934 came the fourth of what are known as golf's 'Majors', with the inauguration of the US Masters.

Unlike the other three Majors, the Masters is played at the same course every year – at the beautiful setting of the Augusta National course in Atlanta. Both the golf course and the tournament were the idea of the legendary Bobby Jones who hailed from Atlanta.

The course was designed by Alister Mackenzie on what had been a nursery developed by a Belgian, Baron Berckmans. The remnants of the days of it being one of the great nurseries of the area are seen in the magnificent array of flowers, shrubs, and trees which adorn the course and contribute towards making it one of the most beautiful settings in golf.

To win the Masters is among the dreams of all professional golfers but many never even get the chance to play in the great event. Participation is by invitation only and based on strict rules, which are amended from time to time. The invitation-only rule was introduced by Jones at the very beginning and has been adhered to ever since.

Entry includes not only a large number of American professionals, but also overseas players and leading amateurs to give the Masters a mixed field, although the quality may not always have been the best that could have been assembled.

Perhaps strangely, the first Masters tournament in 1934 attracted little publicity and was not particularly well supported. Jones even came out of retirement to take part in an effort to attract media and crowd attention. The first championship was won by Horton Smith who snatched a last gasp victory from Craig Wood, but the event was seen as little more than a gathering of Jones and his friends.

However, it gained more publicity in its second year and when Gene Sarazen had a double eagle two at the par-5 15th to stage a remarkable comeback before beating Craig Wood in a 36-hole play-off public interest increased considerably and the Masters became front page news. Wood eventually won the title but had to wait until 1941.

The winner of the Masters receives a coveted green jacket as part of the prize. It is accompanied by a substantial six-figure payout these days. The green jacket is one of the most prestigious prizes in professional golf.

ABOVE: *A birdie and par at the last two holes helped Horton Smith to beat Craig Wood by one stroke to win the first Masters in 1934.*

LEFT: *Gene Sarazen, whose double eagle two at Augusta's 15th in the 1935 Masters is probably one of the most talked about shots in golf.*

RIGHT: *English-born Harry Cooper never won the Masters but was second to Horton Smith in 1936 and joint second behind Henry Picard in 1938.*

LEFT: *Two of the game's greats, Walter Hagen and Bobby Jones, were paired together for the inaugural Masters. Neither lived up to his reputation and they did not figure among the front runners. It would have been nice to see Jones figure prominently because the idea of the Masters emanated from him.*

BELOW: *Gene Sarazen won the Masters at the first attempt in 1935.*

To win the Masters requires four rounds of concentration and accurate driving. Water hazards weave their way around the course and the infamous 'Coffin Corner' in the middle of the back nine has been the downfall of many great players. The greens at Augusta are fast and downhill putts are a nightmare. That is why only the best golfers have won the coveted title ... with a few exceptions of course.

Before Augusta was closed during the war Byron Nelson and Horton Smith had twice mastered the great course to become two-time winners of the title. During the war the course was used initially to graze cattle on to help food production and the war effort. Fortunately it was soon realised that the cattle were destroying the beautiful bushes and trees so the course was changed into a turkey farm instead.

After the war Jimmy Demaret got the better of Augusta with wins in 1947 and 1950 while in 1951 Ben Hogan had the first of his Masters wins, after ten years of trying. When he won the title again two years later he played some of the finest golf ever seen over the course and his four round total of 274 bettered the Masters record by a staggering five strokes.

Gary Player in 1961 was the first non-American winner of the Masters and he has been joined in recent years by Severiano Ballesteros, Bernhard Langer, Sandy Lyle and Nick Faldo.

Arnold Palmer won the first of his four titles in 1958 and Jack Nicklaus won the first of his record six Masters titles in 1963. He was still putting the green jacket on in 1986 at the age of 46. He truly is the Master of Augusta.

Although the British and US Open championships are probably harder to win, the Masters is still perhaps the most prestigious of the four major championships. It can proudly boast the highest standards of sportsmanship among its competitors. That was a feature of Bobby Jones' play and that standard has been maintained.

THE THIRTIES – A GREAT ERA

What a great era the thirties was for golf, particularly in America as some great characters and performers like Gene Sarazen, Ralph Guldahl, Densmore Shute, Olin Dutra, and so on came to the fore.

However, American dominance of the British Open waned in the second half of the decade. They had maintained their grip on the tournament from 1930-33 with wins from Bobby Jones, Tommy Armour, Gene Sarazen and Denny Shute but then Britain's Henry Cotton, the finest British golfer of the era, ended an American run of 11 straight successes with a five stroke win at Sandwich in 1934.

Cotton opened a door for his compatriots and there was not to be another American victory in the British Open throughout the remainder of the thirties. When Cotton won the title a second time at Carnoustie in 1937 it was regarded as one of his finest wins because the entire US Ryder Cup team was in the field. Cotton won by two strokes but that served little as a pointer for the Ryder Cup, for the Americans won again.

Henry Cotton was born in Cheshire in 1907 and turned professional in 1924. His first post was at the age of 19 when he became professional at Langley Park, Beckenham. In 1929 he helped the British Ryder Cup team to its first win over the Americans at Moortown. When he won his first British Open title in 1934 Cotton was based at the Waterloo Club in Belgium. His second round 65 was a new Open record which stood until 1977. Cotton won his third Open title in 1948 to become the only man to win the title both before and after the war. He gave much back to the sport he loved as a teacher and coach at his golf schools in Spain and Portugal. Henry Cotton died in 1987 at the age of 80.

The other stalwarts of British golf in the thirties were the Whitcombe brothers, Ernest, Reg and Charles, the sons of a Burnham (Somerset) gamekeeper. Ernest was the oldest and was runner-up in the Open in 1924. Charles was third in the Open in 1935 but youngest brother Reg managed to do what the other two couldn't – he won the title at Sandwich in 1938, a year after finishing second to Henry Cotton. All three brothers were stalwarts of the Ryder Cup and made ten appearances between them. All three played together in the same side in 1935.

Another great British golfer of the era was Alf Padgham. Born in Surrey he and his family had strong connections with the Royal Ashdown Forest Club and he served his apprenticeship there before taking a post at Sundridge Park. Third in the 1934 British Open at Sandwich, he went one better the following year when he finished runner-up to Alf Perry and at Hoylake in 1936 Alf Padgham became British Open champion for the one and only time. He was also honored with the captaincy of the PGA which made it a memorable year for one of golf's quiet men.

However, it was on the other side of the Atlantic that some great names in golf were making front page news.

The most successful golfer on either side of the Atlantic in the thirties was Gene Sarazen, one of the game's great characters. Sarazen won four majors between 1932-35 and was the first man to win all four majors; British Open, US Open, US PGA and Masters. Born in New York in 1902 he emerged as a great talent along with Walter Hagen and Bob Jones in the 1920s but also became one of the dominant golfers of the next decade. Known affectionately as 'The Squire', he had three majors to his name by the time the thirties arrived and he soon increased that total to seven.

He beat Macdonald Smith by five strokes to win the British Open at Prince's in 1932 and that same year completed a notable double when he won the US Open at Fresh Meadow, with a three stroke margin over Bobby Cruickshank. Sarazen won his third PGA title in 11 years at Milwaukee the following year when he beat Willie Goggin 5 & 4 in the final and in 1935 he won the Masters after a play-off with Craig Wood. Sarazen's double eagle at the par-5 15th on the fourth round remains one of the most talked about golf shots of all time.

ABOVE: *Edinburgh-born Tommy Armour became a naturalized US citizen and in 1927 was the US Open champion. He returned to his native Scotland in 1931 to capture the British Open at Carnoustie.*

LEFT: *Densmore Shute playing out of a bunker at Walton Heath during his £500 challenge match against Britain's Henry Cotton in 1937. Cotton won 6 & 5.*

FAR LEFT: *Ernest Whitcombe, one of three famous golfing brothers. He is seen here in action during the 1924 British Open when he finished runner-up to Walter Hagen, just one stroke behind the great American.*

OPPOSITE PAGE: *Britain's finest golfer both immediately before and after World War II was Henry Cotton, three times winner of the Open.*

ABOVE: *The tall powerful Texan Ralph Guldahl had a remarkable spell in the three years 1937-39 winning the US Open twice and the Masters once.*

ABOVE LEFT: *Charles Whitcombe, a member of six British Ryder Cup teams.*

BELOW LEFT: *A young Dai Rees in 1936.*

When Gene Sarazen made his British Open debut at Troon in 1923 he embarrassingly missed the cut. When he returned to the famous Scottish course 50 years later he holed-in-one at the 'Postage Stamp' 8th. It was one of the most popular aces in British Open history.

Sarazen's total of four major wins was the best haul in the thirties but following close behind with three wins each were Denny Shute and Ralph Guldahl.

Shute was inspired by such men as Sarazen, Hagen and Jones, and turned professional in 1928. He came close to winning the PGA title in 1931 but lost in the final to Sarazen's former caddie Tom Creavy. Shute eventually got his just rewards when he won the 1933 British Open at St Andrews after a play-off with fellow American Craig Wood. Denny's four rounds were 73-73-73-73, the most consistent golf ever played by a British Open champion. The elation of winning the Open made up for the agony in the Ryder Cup two weeks earlier when he missed a return putt on the last green in his singles with Syd Easterbrook which would have halved the match. Instead Great Britain won 6½-5½.

Shute won the PGA title in 1936 by beating Jimmy Thomson 3 & 2 in the final. He beat 'Jug' McSpaden to retain the title the following year. No man has since retained his PGA title. Cleveland-born Shute died in 1974 at the age of 69.

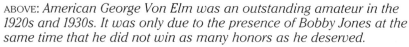

ABOVE: *American George Von Elm was an outstanding amateur in the 1920s and 1930s. It was only due to the presence of Bobby Jones at the same time that he did not win as many honors as he deserved.*

CENTER: *Olin Dutra, winner of the 1934 US Open. The following year he became chairman of the USPGA tournament committee. Sheer dedication took Dutra to the top of golf in the 1930s.*

FAR RIGHT: *Alf Padgham could hit the ball a long way yet had only a short swing. He was also very adept on the putting surface. And at Hoylake in 1936 it came good for him as the quiet man of golf captured the British Open crown.*

America's other 'champion' of the thirties was Ralph Guldahl, winner of the US Open in 1937 and 1938 and Masters champion in 1939; the only man to win a major in three successive years during the decade.

Born in Dallas, Guldahl only spent four years at the top, but what an impact he had in those brief years. He first attracted attention in the 1933 US Open when he had a four-foot putt to tie the championship with amateur Jimmy Goodman. Unfortunately he missed and little more was heard of him until 1936 when he won the Western Open – a high ranking event regarded as a '5th Major' in some people's eyes at the time.

Guldahl retained the Western Open in 1937 and, after throwing away a six shot lead in the Masters, he made up for the disappoint-

ment a couple of months later when he beat Sam Snead, playing in his first Open, by two shots to win at Oakland. Guldahl's total of 281 was a championship record for more than 10 years.

Guldahl continued his excellent run in 1938 when he became the first man to win the Western Open three years in succession. A similar pattern emerged. He was again in second place in the Masters and then, a couple of months later, won the US Open, this time by six strokes from Dick Metz at Cherry Hills. The elusive Masters title eventually came Ralph's way in 1939 when he shot a 33 on the closing nine holes to beat Sam Snead by one stroke.

Surprisingly Ralph Guldahl quit tournament golf shortly after appearing in the 1940 US Open to concentrate on his club professional's job and to spend more time with his family. He had a brief spell at the top, but he was the most successful of all golfers in the second half of the thirties.

Although Sarazen, Guldahl, and Shute were the outstanding golfers in terms of championship successes, there were many other fine golfers who emerged as championship contenders in the 1930s.

There was the twice Masters champion Horton Smith, and the man with the perfect swing, Henry Picard, who won 27 US Tour events between 1934 and 1945. There was also the bespectacled Paul Runyan who twice won the PGA title and later became one of the game's most respected teachers.

And let's not forget that three of the great early post-war champions, Sam Snead, Byron Nelson and Ben Hogan all turned professional in the 1930s, but theirs is a tale to tell separately.

GOLF'S SECOND GREAT TRIUMVIRATE
HOGAN, SNEAD & NELSON

Harry Vardon, James Braid and John H Taylor dominated golf in the early part of the 20th century. They were likened to the Roman leaders Pompey, Caesar and Crassus of two thousand years before and like them were known as 'The Great Triumvirate'.

The golfing world, however, didn't have to wait anything like two thousand years for the coming of its next Triumvirate. Little over twenty years after Braid, Taylor and Vardon ended their domination of the game the next outstanding threesome of Hogan, Nelson and Snead came along.

Like their British predecessors they had a virtual monopoly of top-level success in the game worldwide. But their monopoly, although not lasting as long, must be viewed in a different light because it was at a time when they dominated the four major championships of the world, not just one.

Ben Hogan, Byron Nelson and Sam Snead were all supreme champions in their own right and all three were record breakers. Between 1937 and 1954 they captured no fewer than 21 Major championships between them. It was in the period from 1946-54 that they were dominant, winning 15 of the 36 Majors. And that was at a time when they had such rivals as Jimmy Demaret, Claude Harmon, Lloyd Mangrum, Cary Middlecoff, Julius Boros and Jim Ferrier to contend with.

Coincidentally, all three were born in 1912. The first to turn professional was Byron Nelson who did so in 1932 at the age of 20. Born at Fort Worth, Texas, Nelson worked as a caddie before turning professional. He was a tremendous player with the driver although his putting often let him down.

He won his first Tour event in 1935 when he captured the New Jersey Open and in 1937 he posted notice that a great talent was emerg-

ABOVE: *Byron Nelson with just one of the many trophies he got his hands on in 1946. His record tally of 18 Tour wins the previous season will probably never be beaten or even approached.*

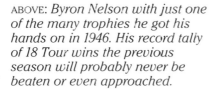

LEFT: *Ryder Cup 1953. Britain's John Panton putts in front of a large crowd during his foursomes match partnered with Eric Brown. However, they were no match for the US captain Sam Snead (waiting to putt) and Lloyd Mangrum who won 5 & 4.*

ing when he pulled back six strokes on Ralph Guldahl in the final round to capture the Masters. In the years leading up to the war Nelson won four Majors including his first and only US Open championship in 1939 when he beat Craig Wood and Denny Shute in a three-way play-off to take the title at the Philadelphia Country Club. Sam Snead had seemingly had the title in his grasp. He came to the 72nd hole needing, it transpired later, a par-5 to win the title. He took an eight and finished fifth. Snead was never to win the US Open during his long and distinguished career.

Nelson followed up his Open success by beating Snead by one hole to win the PGA Championship in 1940 to make amends for his defeat at the 37th by Henry Picard a year earlier. The match-play format of the PGA in those days suited Nelson's style of play and he was runner-up again in 1941 when Vic Ghezzi beat him at the 38th hole.

He won his fourth Major in six years in 1942 when he won the Masters for a second time, beating fellow Texan Ben Hogan by five strokes in the first 18-hole play off in Masters history.

Bryon Nelson won one more major during the remainder of his

LEFT: *Ben Hogan (right) and Sam Snead were the United States representatives in the 1956 Canada (now World) Cup. They captured the trophy with Hogan winning the individual title.*

RIGHT: *Ben Hogan (right) sharing a joke with top amateur Billy Joe Patton who finished third behind Snead and Hogan in the 1954 Masters.*

BELOW: *A happy Ben Hogan after beating Mike Turnesa 7 & 6 in the final to win the 1948 PGA championship at Norwood Hills, Missouri.*

career. But he engraved his name in the record books in 1944 and 1945 when he won a remarkable 26 US Tour events. But that's another story.

Sam Snead, however, is the champion when it comes to winning on the US Tour and has more wins to his name than any other man.

Born at Hot Springs, Virginia, he turned professional in 1933 but was still making a name for himself while Byron Nelson was coming to the peak of his career. But while Nelson, and his other great rival of the day, Ben Hogan, drifted away from the professional scene in the 1950s, Sam Snead kept on playing, and kept on winning. Snead was the last link between the Triumvirate of Hogan, Nelson and Snead, and the next great golfing trio, Palmer, Player and Nicklaus.

Snead won seven majors, but he was never to win the US Open despite finishing runner-up no fewer than four times. He won his first

major in 1942 when he beat Jim Turnesa 2 & 1 to win the PGA Championship at Seaview, New Jersey, and in 1946 he won the first post-war British Open when he beat fellow American Johnny Bulla and the South African Bobby Locke by four strokes at St Andrews. A year later he was beaten by Lew Worsham by one stroke in the play-off for the US Open at St Louis Country Club. Snead missed a putt from less than three feet at the 18th. This defeat came exactly ten years after his Open debut when he was also runner-up. After such an auspicious start in the Open one would have thought that one day the title would be his but he was to go through his long career without ever getting his hands on the trophy. However, there were the other majors, and Snead had his fair share of them.

Majors numbers three and four came his way in 1949 when he had two closing rounds of 67 to beat Johnny Bulla by three strokes to capture the Masters title and then beat Johnny Palmer to win the PGA title at Richmond, Virginia, his home state. Snead won his third PGA title two years later when he became the then oldest winner of the title, at 39, after an easy 7 & 6 success over Walter Burkemo at Oakmont. The following year, 1952, Snead took Masters title number two when he finished four strokes ahead of Jack Burke. Two years later, at the age of 42, he won his third Masters title when he beat his great rival Hogan by one stroke in an 18-hole play-off. It was Sam Snead's last major success but he kept on winning on the US Tour until 1965.

So to the final member of golf's second great triumvirate, Ben Hogan, the man with the perfect swing. A great stylist, Hogan was born at Dublin, Texas, and turned professional in 1931. Like Snead, he was still learning his profession while Byron Nelson was coming to his peak. Hogan's glory days were to come in the immediate post-war years when his superiority was unquestioned. He was a tremendous stroke player with great concentration and determination. He also had the copy book swing.

Hogan had the best record of the Triumvirate with nine Majors to his credit including three in 1953; the only instance of a professional winning three majors in one season.

Despite his future success it was not until eight years after he turned professional in 1931 that Ben Hogan won his first Tour event, the Hershey Fourball. It was to be another two years before his second win but in the three years 1940-42 he topped the money list each year. Hogan's best years, however, were to come after the war. In 1946 he had 13 wins, a figure bettered only by Byron Nelson the previous year, this was also the year that he captured his first major when he took the PGA title by beating 'Porky' Oliver 6 & 4 at Portland,

ABOVE: *The second 'great Triumvirate' were occasionally threatened by other top US stars during their 'reign' and one man capable of upsetting the odds was former night club singer Jimmy Demaret, three times winner of the Masters.*

RIGHT: *For so long Craig Wood was destined to be the 'nearly man'. But it all came good in 1941 when he won the Masters and US Open titles. He is seen here with the Open trophy.*

LEFT: *Paul Runyan beat Sam Snead 8 & 7 in the 1937 PGA Championship final. It was the biggest winning margin in the final during the championship's spell as a match-play event. Runyan later became an excellent golf teacher.*

Oregon. Two years later he won the US Open/PGA double. His Open win, at the Riveira, was with a championship record 276 and was two strokes better than Jimmy Demaret, who also beat the old record. When he won the PGA title at Norwood Hills a few months later Hogan had plenty to spare when he beat Mike Turnesa 7 & 6.

He missed most of the 1949 season following a bad automobile accident but made a remarkable comeback to win the US Open at Merion in 1950, won the US Open and Masters the following year and then, in 1953, he won the US Open, British Open and Masters. By

rights Hogan shouldn't have won any more majors. Firstly he was given up for dead following the accident. And then he was told he probably wouldn't walk again. And certainly wouldn't play golf again. But he did.

Between them Ben Hogan, Byron Nelson and Sam Snead won exactly 200 US Tour events. Nicklaus, Palmer and Player have won 153 to date. Both trios have been outstanding in their own eras. Golf always needs great players. The 1940s and early 1950s were fortunate enough to have three of them simultaneously.

NELSON'S REMARKABLE SEASON

Byron Nelson won eight Tour events in 1944 to beat Sam Snead's record of seven set in 1938. But Texan Nelson had even more to offer the following season when he won a staggering 18 tournaments including a remarkable run of 11 consecutive wins.

The media were quick to point out, however, that, because he was a haemophiliac, Nelson was exempt from military service unlike some of the other leading professionals of the day. Despite the absence of some of the top players, it must be remembered that Sam Snead provided much of Nelson's opposition during the season and he also won six Tour events. For Nelson to beat Snead in so many events, and then string together his remarkable run of success was no mean feat. Furthermore he put together a sequence of 19 successive rounds under 70. It doesn't matter who you are playing, a run like that is certainly impressive.

His amazing season started as early as 14 January when he beat Denny Shute by two strokes to win the Phoenix Open. When he won the Miami Four Ball at Miami Springs on 11 March it was his fourth Tour win of the season. Significantly, it was to herald the start of that remarkable run of 11 successive Tour wins.

In the four consecutive weeks after his win at Miami with Jug McSpaden, he won the Charlotte Open, Greensboro Open, Durham Open and Atlanta Open. His next tournament, and indeed victory, came in Canada when he won the Montreal Open on 10 June and between then and 4 August he won every tournament he entered – the Philadelphia Inquirer Invitational, Chicago Victory National Open, PGA Championship, Tam O'Shanter Open and finally the Canadian Open at Toronto.

His PGA success came at Morraine Country Club, Ohio. It was his

LEFT: *Byron Nelson's record of 18 wins in a season, 11 of them consecutive, will both be US Tour records well into the 21st century. He is seen here in action during the qualifying rounds for the 1955 British Open at St Andrews.*

ABOVE: *Nelson (right) with Sam Snead both have their hands on the PGA trophy in 1940. But it was Nelson who took it home after his 1 hole win.*

RIGHT: *The 1940 PGA victory made up for his defeat at the 37th by Henry Picard (left) the year before.*

fifth final in six years. He gained an emphatic victory over Sam Byrd by 4 & 3 to win his fifth, and final major.

Two weeks after winning the Canadian Open, Nelson took part in the Memphis Open. He finished joint fourth behind winner Fred Haas and thus came to an end one of the greatest winning sequences in golf history. But it was back to winning ways the following week when he took the Knoxville Invitational. He added three more titles before the year was out as he improved the Tour record for wins in a season from 8 to 18. That record still stands and is five more than the next best total, established by Ben Hogan in 1946. In addition to his 11 wins in succession, Nelson also won a 12th tournament during the sequence but this was not an official Tour event as the prize money was below the tour minimum.

Not surprisingly Nelson shattered the US Tour record for prizemoney in a season with a total of $63,335 (paid in War Bonds). It was certainly a record breaking season for Byron Nelson.

He lost the 1946 US Open after a three way play off involving Vic Ghezzi and winner Lloyd Mangrum. In 1947 he was joint second in the Masters behind the champion Jimmy Demaret.

Nelson was not to come close to winning a major again but he carried on winning on the US Tour until 1951 when he ended his career with a total of 54 Tour wins, the fifth best of all time. During the war years he went 113 consecutive tournaments without missing the cut. No matter what Byron Nelson will be remembered for, his 18 wins in one season, 11 of them in succession, will take pride of place above all his other achievements.

SLAMMIN' SAM'S GREAT CAREER

Sam Snead, known affectionately as 'Slammin' Sam,' not only won seven majors but also won 84 US Tour events, more than any other man in golfing history. Jack Nicklaus is currently second to Snead with 71 wins, but is unlikely to overtake Sam's great total.

The man from White Sulphur Springs, Virginia, won his first professional event, the Virginia Closed Championship in 1936 at the age of 25. When he won his 84th and last event, the 1965 Greater Greensboro Open, he was 52 years and 10 months old. He remains the oldest winner of a US Tour event. Remarkably it was Snead's eighth Greater Greensboro Open win. No other man has won any single US event as often.

Nobody else has enjoyed such a long career on the US Tour as Snead and well after his last Tour win he was still breaking records.

In 1974 he finished joint third in the PGA Championship at Tanglewood when only Jack Nicklaus and Lee Trevino had better scores. His performance elevated him to 49th on the money list that year, a remarkable achievement for a 62-year-old. A further astonishing feat came in the 1979 Quad Cities Open when he was 67 and managed to shoot a round of 66 to become the first man on the Tour to shoot or better his own age.

His first season on the US Tour was in 1937 when he won four titles and finished third on the money list but the following season he topped the list with $19,534 after winning a then record seven tournaments, including the 'fifth' major, the Canadian Open.

Between his debut season and 1953 he never finished lower than 18th on the money list and topped it again on two more occasions, in

1949 and 1950 when he won a total of 16 tournaments. His best tally from one season was 10 in 1950 and although he never came close to matching Nelson's 1945 feat of 11 consecutive wins, he did, that same 1945 season, win three consecutive tournaments, a feat achieved by only a handful of golfers on the Tour. When he won the US Vardon Trophy in 1950 he did so with an average of 69.23 strokes. This remains a Tour record.

He has twice recorded successive rounds aggregating 126 strokes, both one time Tour records. In the 1950 Texas Open he shot consecutive rounds of 63 and in the 1957 Dallas Open his two middle rounds were 60 and 66. His 60 equalled the US Tour record at the time.

Although he has not played on the US Tour regularly since 1979 Sam Snead was a popular figure on the US Seniors Tour and whenever he turns out he remains one of the most popular men in golf.

He has been credited with 135 wins worldwide and in addition to his 84 wins on the US Tour he played on seven winning Ryder Cup teams and three winning US World Cup (Canada Cup) teams. He also won the individual title in 1961.

Sam Snead had one of the finest of golf swings and it was that swing which made him a winner for more than 30 years.

FAR LEFT: *The majestically fluent swing of Sam Snead. It was that swing which kept him playing at the highest level for many years.*

LEFT: *. . . and his swing seen from behind. The poise and balance are perfect.*

TOP LEFT: *Snead is presented with the British Open trophy after his fine four stroke win in the first post-war championship, at St Andrews.*

ABOVE: *Sam Snead in 1937, his first year on the Tour. He looks apprehensive as he looks at his card.*

HOGAN'S WONDERFUL RECOVERY

On a foggy Texas morning on 2 February 1949, Ben Hogan and his wife Valerie were returning to their Fort Worth home by car. Suddenly a bus appeared and a head-on collision was imminent. In an act of bravery Hogan flung himself across his wife to protect her, which he did.

As people gathered around the twisted wreck of Hogan's car it suddenly dawned upon them who the illustrious driver was and cries of 'he's dead' soon circulated around the crowd. Mercifully, Ben Hogan was not dead but he had suffered multiple injuries.

After undergoing surgery doctors told him there was a possibility he would not walk again and as for playing golf, there was no chance. But Ben Hogan had guts and determination and less than a year after the horrific accident he was competing in the Los Angeles Open.

Still hobbling, Hogan had made the trip to England in the fall of 1949 to captain the US Ryder Cup team and he led them to their fourth consecutive success. The following January he entered the Los Angeles Open to see if he could stand up to the rigors of tournament golf again around Riviera's 7029 yards, the scene of Hogan's first US Open win in 1948. He astounded many people, and probably himself as well, when he finished the four rounds on 280 and tied first place with Sam Snead. Unfortunately, Ben lost the play-off but he showed once again what great character he possessed.

Five months later, and a mere 16 months after coming from the edge of death, Ben Hogan defied the doctors to pull off one of the greatest comebacks ever seen in golfing history when he captured the US Open title. Many asked whether Hogan would be able to stand up to so much pressure or indeed, if he could physically drag himself around 72 holes at Merion for what was the 50th US Open championship. Particularly testing was the requirement to play 36 holes on the final day.

That surely should have been too much for Hogan, but no. He shot rounds of 72 and 74 to get into a three-way play-off with Lloyd Mangrum and George Fazio. But another 18 holes followed the next day and to everybody's surprise and delight, except for Mangrum and Fazio of course, Hogan finished with a 69 to the 73 and 75 of his respective opponents.

Hogan's victory was one of the most emotional wins in the history of US golf but the remarkable career of Ben Hogan did not end there. The winning continued. He successfully defended his Open title in 1951 when he 'brought the monster to its knees,' a reference to the tough Oakland Hills course. Hogan shot a magnificent last round 67 to beat Clayton Heafner by two shots. He always maintained that 67 was one of the finest rounds of golf he ever played. Many golf commentators would regard it, moreover, as one of the best rounds ever played by any golfer. One measure of its quality was that the only other player to beat the par of 70 throughout the tournament was the runner up Clayton Heafner with his last round 69.

Hogan also took the first of two Masters titles in 1951 after several times coming close to winning the coveted prize. A final round 68 was good enough to ensure a two stroke win over Skee Riegel. But Hogan was still not finished. He had better things to come.

After a blank year in 1952, although he finished third in the US Open at Northwood, he took the golf world by storm in 1953 when he won three professional majors, something no man had achieved before, or since. Hogan had not appeared in three majors in one season since 1948, the year before his accident, but in 1953 he competed in the Masters, US Open, and in the British Open, for the first, and only, time.

The Masters was the first title to come Hogan's way and he took the title with the best sustained four rounds of golf he ever played. He strung together rounds of 70, 69, 66, and 69. It was the first time any man had three rounds under 70 at Augusta. Hogan won by five shots

RIGHT: *The classic swing of Ben Hogan. These pictures were taken shortly before his return to competitive golf after his accident. They clearly show he had lost none of his fluency . . . and that was after being told he wouldn't walk again!*

LEFT: *As the non-playing captain of the 1949 US Ryder Cup team Hogan accepts the trophy after the Americans had retained the cup with a 7-5 win at Ganton, Yorkshire. Two years earlier Hogan captained the side to an 11-1 victory on home soil.*

OVERLEAF: *Ben Hogan in action during the 1956 Canada Cup.*

ABOVE: *Ben Hogan (left) with his wife Valerie and film star Glenn Ford, who portrayed Hogan in the film* Follow the Sun, *the only feature film about the life of a professional golfer.*

BELOW: *Australian-born Jim Ferrier, a regular competitor in the US in the 40s and 50s, was the 1947 USPGA champion.*

from runner-up Porky Oliver, and by eight shots from the third man Lloyd Mangrum.

He followed his Masters success by emulating Willie Anderson and Bob Jones in winning his fourth US Open (in six years). The championship was played at Oakmont, and Hogan led the tournament throughout. He ended up with a four round total of 283 and won by six strokes from Sam Snead, the biggest winning margin since Ralph Guldahl's six-stroke win over Dick Metz at Cherry Hills in 1938.

But it was at Carnoustie, venue of the British Open, that Hogan received one of the finest welcomes a visiting American golfer had ever received in Britain. After his accident Hogan was not too keen on traveling but was persuaded to make the journey to Scotland to appear in his first British Open. Crowds turned out by their thousands and many of them were willing the American to win. Having never previously played in the Open Hogan was surprised at how popular he was with the British fans. He did not disappoint and had improving rounds of 73, 71, 70 and 68 to win by four strokes from fellow American, the amateur, Frank Stranahan, Australian Peter Thomson, Argentinian Tony Cerda, and Britain's Dai Rees.

In winning the British Open Hogan emulated Gene Sarazen in winning all four Majors. Sadly, the PGA Championship clashed with the British Open in 1953 and this prevented Hogan having a chance of achieving the ultimate Grand Slam. However, it should be said that Hogan did not have a great love of match-play golf, and often missed the US PGA event.

Nevertheless, his remarkable achievement of three Majors in 1953 is one that has remained unbeaten nearly forty years later despite the presence of some great golfers in the intervening years. But Ben Hogan's real triumph was in coming back on to a golf course at all after his accident on that foggy day in February 1949. He had always had a perfect golf swing and fortunately the accident never took that away from him. It was that swing which took him to the top in the first place and it was that swing that helped him return as one of the most remarkable and finest golfers of all time.

RIGHT: *Jimmy Demaret was runner-up to his fellow Texan Ben Hogan in the 1948 US Open.*

LEFT: *Julius Boros spoilt Hogan's possible run of four successive US Open titles by winning the championship in 1952; Hogan had to be content with third place, five shots off the lead.*

THE FIRST GREAT AUSTRALIAN
PETER THOMSON

Before the war Australia's top player was the amateur Jim Ferrier. Although born in New South Wales he emigrated to the United States during the war and became a professional. At the time of his climb up the professional ladder in the immediate post-war years, another Australian talent was emerging in the shape of Norman Von Nida. But both men were put in the shadow by Peter Thomson, widely regarded as the first great Australian professional.

Born in Melbourne in 1929 he started playing on his own at a local course during the war. He had no professional advice yet built a swing that was to hold him in good stead throughout his career.

He turned professional in 1949 when only 19 and won his first professional tournament, the New Zealand Open in 1950. In 1951 he won the Australian Open championship at the Metropolitan course. However because of the lack of regular competition he made the long trip to Britain to get the chance of regular tournament play and on his British Open debut at Portrush that year he finished joint 6th, eight strokes adrift of the champion Max Faulkner. A year later Thomson was only one stroke behind the winner Bobby Locke.

ABOVE: *One of Peter Thomson's great rivals in the 1950s was South Africa's Bobby Locke. Between them the two Colonials won eight British Open titles between 1949-58.*

LEFT: *A delighted Peter Thomson (center) after winning the British Open title for a second successive year, at St Andrews in 1955. He is flanked by the second placed Johnny Fallon (right), and third placed Frank Jowle.*

Joint second again at Carnoustie in 1953, Peter Thomson was ready to launch an attack on the British Open, the likes of which had not been seen since the days of Braid, Taylor and Vardon.

The first of five triumphs came at Royal Birkdale in 1954 when he beat Sid Scott, Dai Rees and Bobby Locke by one stroke. The South African Locke was Thomson's big rival of the day and in the ten years from 1949-58 they won the Open eight times between them. But it was the Australian who ended up with the best record, with five wins to Locke's eventual tally of four. Thomson retained his title at St Andrews in 1955 and at Hoylake a year later beat the top Belgian Flory van Donck by three shots to become the first man since Bob Ferguson in 1880-82 to win the title three years in succession. No man has since equalled that feat.

RIGHT: *It wasn't to be Thomson's year at Royal Lytham in 1952. He finished second to Bobby Locke seen here receiving the British Open trophy.*

LEFT: *Peter Thomson developed a basic and fluent swing which was to hold him in good stead for many years and take him to five British Open titles, a modern-day record equalled in recent times by Tom Watson.*

RIGHT: *A rare home success in the British Open was Fred Daly's 1947 win at Hoylake.*

BELOW: *Thomson finished joint sixth in his first British Open at Portrush in 1951. The winner was England's Max Faulkner, seen here driving during the 1953 Ryder Cup.*

Many felt Thomson's wins were 'hollow' because of the lack of American competition in the British Open fields at the time. But, while his excellent long-iron game was more suited to British courses than those in the States, he did, in 1956, show the Americans that he could beat their best golfers when he captured the Texas Open, his only win on the US Tour.

Even though the Americans were notable for their absence from the British Open in the 1950s Thomson still had some formidable opposition in Locke, Britain's Dai Rees, Eric Brown, and Harry Weetman, the Belgian van Donck, and an emerging talent from South Africa, Gary Player.

Thomson was deposed as Open champion in 1957 by Locke, who won by three strokes at St Andrews. But the following year, at Lytham, Thomson was the Open 'king' once more when he beat Britain's Dave Thomas by four strokes in a 36-hole play-off.

But those pundits who belittled Thomson's previous four Open wins had to eat their words in 1965 when he won from a field containing not only the best of British, European and South African golfers, but also contained a strong American field, including the defending champion 'Champagne' Tony Lema. Thomson trailed Lema by six strokes after the first round but eventually won by two

strokes and became the first man to win the Open twice at Birkdale.

It was his finest performance in the Open and he joined James Braid and J H Taylor as five times winner of the world's best known championship. Only Harry Vardon has more victories than those three and since Thomson's glory days, only Tom Watson has notched up five wins.

Thomson maintained his winning ways in regular British tournaments throughout the sixties and was third when Tony Jacklin won the Open at Lytham in 1969. He also played a big role in the development of golf in the Far East.

He quit tournament play in 1979 with more than 50 tournament wins worldwide to his name, including the Australian Open in 1972 when he was 43. On reaching the age of 50 Thomson joined the US Seniors Tour and he delighted those American galleries who, 25 years earlier, thought he wasn't good enough to win in the States. He enjoyed great success and won far more money than he ever did in his days as a regular tournament professional.

Since those great days in the 1950s, Australia has produced some notable champions like Kel Nagle, David Graham and Greg Norman. But none has yet managed to scale the heights that five-times Open winner Thomson reached.

A BRITISH RYDER CUP WIN

The poor British had taken quite a hammering at their 'own' game since Francis Ouimet gave heart to his fellow Americans.

In the period between the two World Wars American golfers had won the British Open 12 times including ten in succession 1924-33. After World War II Sam Snead made it another victory for the States but then there was a decline in interest from the western side of the Atlantic. However, British golfers were still put in the shadow by the likes of Bobby Locke and Peter Thomson. By 1957 there had been only three post-war British winners of the Open. As for the Ryder Cup, well, Britain was certainly kept in her place by the Americans who had dominated the event since 1935 and had not lost since the one point defeat for Walter Hogan's team at Southport and Ainsdale in 1933.

Since then Walter Hagen, Ben Hogan, Sam Snead, Lloyd Mangrum and Chick Harbert had all skippered winning American teams. Only Mangrum, at Wentworth in 1953, received anything like a scare when the margin of victory was only one point.

Jack Burke had the honor of skippering the American team which made the trip to Lindrick near Sheffield, Yorkshire, in 1957. Britain's captain was Dai Rees, a Ryder Cup player for 20 years. The Americans were favorites. Well they would be with a record of played 11, won 9, lost 2. After the first day's foursomes their odds improved.

ABOVE; *Art Wall (seen here) and his partner Fred Hawkins were the United States' only losers in the foursomes at Lindrick. Wall was left out of the singles while Hawkins played and was the only US winner.*

RIGHT: *Ken Bousfield (pictured) and Dai Rees were Britain's only winners in both foursomes and singles.*

LEFT: *This is how* Golf *magazine captured Max Faulkner's 1951 Open success.*

Jack Burke

Peter Alliss and Bernard Hunt were beaten 2 & 1 by Doug Ford and Dow Finsterwald before Ken Bousfield and Dai Rees levelled the score with a 3 & 2 win over Art Wall and Fred Hawkins, but that was to be Britain's only success on the first day. Max Faulkner and Harry Weetman were soundly beaten by Jack Burke and Ted Kroll, 4 & 3, and Christy O'Connor and Eric Brown suffered an even heavier defeat at the hands of Dick Mayer and Tommy Bolt, 7 & 5.

Trailing 3-1 at the end of the first day left the very large crowd thinking that another defeat was imminent. But the British team came out for the second day's singles with renewed heart and confidence.

They had suffered enough defeats. Now it was time to put the records straight. But what a mountain they had to climb.

Eric Brown led the way with a 4 & 3 win over Bolt and when Peter Mills beat the US skipper Jack Burke by 5 & 3 it not only made it a remarkable Ryder Cup debut for the 27-year-old Mills but levelled the match at 3-all. Peter Alliss had the misfortune of being the only Briton to lose his singles when he was beaten 2 & 1 by Fred Hawkins but Ken Bousfield made sure the match remained in the balance with a 4 & 3 win over Lionel Hebert. Elsewhere on the course Bousfield's team-mates were building up big leads and suddenly the crowd was get-

LEFT: *The American skipper Jack Burke. It wasn't a happy occasion for him, since he became the first US captain since Walter Hagen in 1933 to lead a losing team.*

RIGHT: *Dai Rees led the Britain team by example. He won his foursomes match with Ken Bousfield and then comprehensively beat Ed Furgol 7 & 6 in the singles.*

BELOW: *The smile from Welshman Dai Rees (left) says it all: 'We've got it back at last'. But sadly it didn't stay in British hands for long and it would be 28 years before the Americans were beaten again. Rees' teammate Eric Brown (right) looks on.*

RIGHT: *Ed Furgol seems pretty happy here, but he wasn't too happy at Lindrick in 1957: he lost his only match 7 & 6 when beaten by the British captain Dai Rees.*

BELOW: *For Peter Alliss, seen here in action in 1964, the 1957 Ryder Cup was a tournament he would like to forget; he was the only member of the British team to lose in the singles. Fortunately it had no bearing on the final result.*

RIGHT: *Harry Weetman appeared in his fourth Ryder Cup in 1957. After defeat in the foursomes he was left out of the singles.*

ting excited. A British win looked a distinct possibility and as the scores were posted, it was one win after the other for the British lads.

Dai Rees gained a magnificent 7 & 6 win over Ed Furgol and Bernard Hunt's 6 & 5 win over Ford was equally impressive. And when Christy O'Connor reached the 12th tee he was virtually un-beatable and had the match in the bag. He confirmed it with a 7 & 6 win over Finsterwald. Harry Bradshaw halved the last match with

Dick Meyer and Britain had won the Ryder Cup for the first time in 24 years.

The win was felt to be the 'shot in the arm' British golf needed but oh dear, how wrong everybody was. The Americans reasserted their hold on the Ryder Cup two years later and, as for British Open suc-cesses, the home fans had to wait until 1969. For the next Ryder Cup win the wait was to be even longer.

THANKS ARNIE

Arnold Palmer has done so much for golf in more than 35 years since he turned pro. His fellow professionals owe him a huge debt for his role in bringing big money into the game but the British public, and the golf world in general, also owe him a great big 'thank you' for his personal drive in maintaining the standard of the British Open which was starting to decline in the late 1950s.

From the moment Jock Hutchinson won the Open at St Andrews in 1921 until 1933, American golfers dominated Britain's senior golf tournament. But since Denny Shute's win at St Andrews in 1933 the only American wins had been by Sam Snead in 1946 and Ben Hogan in 1953. By the end of the 1950s American professionals were not bothering to make the trip across the Atlantic. The moving of the Ryder Cup schedule from its traditional June date, when played in Britain, to September, meant two trips in Ryder Cup years for the

ABOVE: *Kel Nagle of Australia won the 1960 Centenary British Open. It was Arnie Palmer's debut in the tournament and he finished second. But his presence helped revive declining interest in the event from his fellow Americans.*

RIGHT: *Palmer in 1967. As usual he attracted a large gallery and that has been the case for more than 30 years.*

ABOVE: *Thanks to Palmer's interest in the Open the great event saw such characters as 'Champagne' Tony Lema, the 1964 champion, make the trip across the Atlantic.*

BELOW: *Palmer during the 1966 US Open; he threw away a seven stroke lead in the final round.*

FAR RIGHT: *One of the game's great sportsmen, Roberto de Vicenzo.*

Americans if they wanted to compete in the Open. Many simply didn't bother.

The lack of American interest, however, was not to the advantage of the British professionals because the championship was dominated by two men from Commonwealth countries; Bobby Locke of South Africa and Peter Thomson of Australia. They won eight titles between them in the years 1949-58. Gary Player also flew the flag for South Africa in 1959 but the following year was the centenary Open and it looked as though there was again to be a poor turn out from the Americans.

However, one man wanted to play his part in reviving US interest. And that man was Arnie Palmer. A professional since 1954, Palmer came to St Andrews for the Centenary Open having already won the US Masters and US Open. He wanted to emulate the great Ben Hogan and win all three in the one year and, also like Hogan, had the desire to win the Open at the first attempt.

Sadly for Palmer it was not to be, and the honor of winning the Centenary championship went to Australian Kel Nagle who beat Palmer by just one stroke. But Palmer had set the wheels in motion. He returned the following year to Birkdale where he won the title by one stroke from Britain's Dai Rees and his play in a near gale in the second round was one of the finest 18 holes he every played. A year after his Birkdale success Palmer was champion again, this time at Troon, and it was sweet revenge because he beat Nagle by six strokes. This was the biggest winning margin since Walter Hagen beat John Farrell in 1929 and Palmer's four round total of 276 was a championship record which stood until beaten by Tom Watson and Jack Nicklaus at Turnberry in 1977.

Palmer's victories were not just about his brilliant play and low scoring. His appearance at Troon saw fans flock to the course in

RIGHT: *Despite beating Britain's Dai Rees by one stroke to win the 1961 British Open at Birkdale, Arnold Palmer was a popular winner.*

BELOW: *Arnold Palmer being watched by his army of fans affectionately known as 'Arnie's Army' during the 1964 World Match-Play Championship at Wentworth. Palmer beat Neil Coles in the final to become the first winner of the championship.*

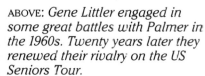

ABOVE: *Gene Littler engaged in some great battles with Palmer in the 1960s. Twenty years later they renewed their rivalry on the US Seniors Tour.*

RIGHT: *Another of Palmer's keen rivals was Gay Brewer, the man with the very distinctive looping swing.*

their thousands. Marshals and stewards had never previously encountered anything like it at the championship. But Arnie's contribution to the British Open went even further than providing crowd-pulling golf. He went back to America after his appearance in the 1960 Centenary Open and 'banged the drum' for the oldest and finest golf championship in the world. His fellow professionals listened and started, albeit gradually at first, to make the trip across the Atlantic every summer.

Palmer has not won the British Open since that day in Troon but, in the 27 championships since then, 15 of his fellow countrymen have won the title and such men as Tom Watson, Jack Nicklaus, and Lee Trevino have become household names among British golf fans. Without Arnie opening the door nearly thirty years ago we might never have been privileged to see them grace the oldest golf tournament in the world.

Sadly for the British fans, the revived interest of US professionals meant a barren time for British golf. Tony Jacklin had a rare moment of British success at Lytham in 1969 and in the eighties both Nick Faldo and Sandy Lyle have played their role in providing a moment of joy for the home support. But they are still quick to applaud and acknowledge the skills of the many great American golfers that have added their name to the famous trophy.

The Open is still regarded as the world's toughest competition to win. Had Arnie not played his part in rekindling its interest among his fellow American professionals in the early sixties, it could well have lost its status as one of the world's top tournaments. Thank you Arnie.

BIG NAMES – BIG MONEY

By the early sixties, Arnold Palmer was the best known golfer in the world. He had not only regenerated American interest in the British Open but had become the man the ordinary club golfer identified himself with. Consequently there was an upsurge in the game's popularity, not only in America, but worldwide.

Palmer was quick to take advantage of the growth area and along with marketing whizz-kid Mark McCormack, set about marketing Arnold Palmer . . . and the game of golf.

Naturally, both men made a lot of money out of the operation, and quite rightly so. But more importantly they made a lot of money for golf and today's professionals should never lose sight of that fact. Had it not been for Palmer's golfing talent and McCormack's equally shrewd business brain, there is little doubting that professional golf in Europe and America would be nowhere near as financially sound as it is today as leading players look to season's winnings with at least five noughts tagged on the end of the first figure.

Palmer is now way down the all-time US money list but on 21 July 1968 he became the first man to have won $1 million on the US Tour. It was appropriate that he should have been the first one to have benefitted from his lead. Since then men like Nicklaus, Kite, Watson and Strange have all gone on to approach or surpass the magical $5 million mark. But today, you don't have to be a great champion to make a lot of money on the US Tour. You do, however, have to be more than just an ordinary golfer. Good Tour players can win over a million dollars in a career without ever winning a tournament. Consistent golf is well rewarded on the Tour and that has only been possible as a result of sponsors wanting to associate themselves with the great game.

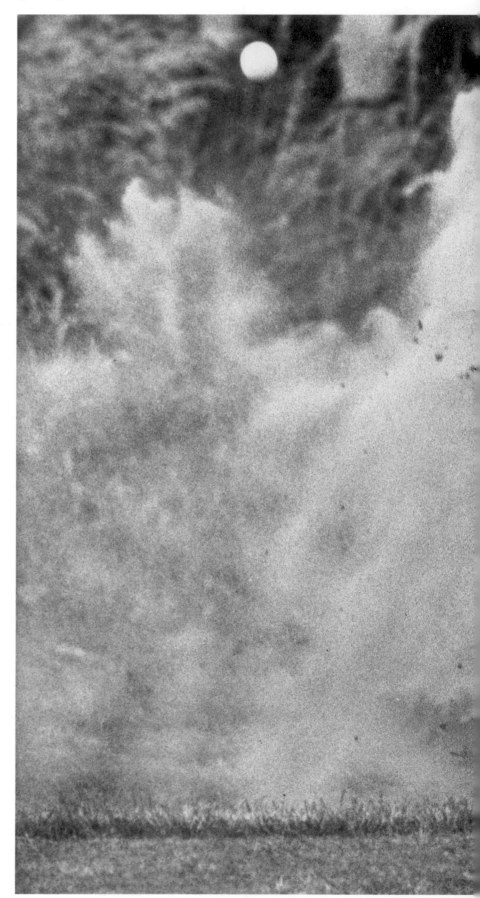

LEFT: *Roberto de Vicenzo (left) reflects on what might have been at the 1968 Masters. He inadvertently signed for a 4 at the 71st hole when he actually shot a 3. He lost by one stroke to Bob Goalby (right). It was a costly error.*

BOTTOM, FAR LEFT: *Bob Charles ponders a putt. Few could match his abilities on the green.*

BELOW: *Orville Moody turned professional in 1967, won the US Open two years later and didn't win another Tour event . . .*

ABOVE: *Roberto de Vicenzo, still in a contemplating mood.*

RIGHT: *Raymond Floyd joined the US Tour in 1963. More than 20 years later he was still winning tournaments.*

BELOW: *Billy Casper was one of the biggest names in world golf in the 1960s. He arrived at approximately the same time as Arnold Palmer and went on to win 51 Tour events, a figure bettered by only five men.*

ABOVE: *The pick of the top Americans came to Birkdale for the 1965 Ryder Cup. Included in their line up were Arnold Palmer, Julius Boros, Tony Lema, Gene Littler, Billy Casper, Ken Venturi, and others.*

LEFT: *Sponsors helped generate the big money that flooded into golf in the 1960s. And today marketing has a big role in the sport. Is that a lifesize bottle of beer with the diminutive Ian Woosnam? Or is it a lifesize Woosnam with a big bottle?*

RIGHT: *New Zealander Bob Charles is regarded as the finest left-handed golfer of all time. His putting skills were a treat to watch.*

The rise of Palmer coincided with television interest in Tour events. And, of course, television coverage is like a magnet to potential sponsors. To give an idea how the game has gained financially because of sponsor involvement, we can look back to 1960 when the US Tour consisted of 41 events giving total purses of $1,335,242. In 1988 the number of events was little more, at 47, but prize money had increased to a staggering $36,959,307.

The influx of money inevitably brought a greater interest in the game and inevitably there would be new names appearing on leader boards at championships across the United States. Consequently Palmer had to make way for up-and-coming stars like Jack Nicklaus, Lee Trevino, Raymond Floyd, Hale Irwin, Johnny Miller, Tom Watson, and countless more who have all benefitted from Palmer's innovations.

In Europe it is the same story. Bernard Hunt was the top British money winner in 1962 with £4492 (then approximately $10,800). In 1988 Seve Ballesteros topped the list with £502,000 ($800,000). The European PGA Tour has been in existence since 1975 when total

prizemoney totalled £700,000. In 1988 the prizemoney went past the £10 million mark for the first time and in 1989 it was £13.25 million ($21.2 million). In 1987 the European PGA signed a sponsorship deal with Volvo cars and the Tour is now known as the Volvo Tour.

The Volvo deal is just one way in which sponsorship can help. The other most common is by having each individual tournament sponsored. But manufacturers of golf equipment, clothing and many other items are also willing to lend their name to professional players. Naturally, the more successful the player, the bigger the payment involved. But lesser known professionals also benefit from golf's high standing in the world of sport and lesser known companies are prepared to support lesser known players in the hope that one day they will have that big break and make it among the elite of the golfing world. Thankfully, golf is one of those games that allows talent to come through. It is not a closed shop and the door is open for players to emerge from the pack to become a champion.

Champions now reap great rewards indeed but it is largely thanks to the efforts of Arnold Daniel Palmer.

THE NEXT GREAT TRIUMVIRATE
PALMER, PLAYER & NICKLAUS

Golf has been fortunate. It has rarely had a spell without a superstar to dominate the game and on three occasions it has been dominated by a trio of superstars. At the turn of the century there was the first Great Triumvirate of Braid, Taylor and Vardon and in the forties and fifties we had Hogan, Nelson and Snead. And then came along the next great threesome of Arnold Palmer, Gary Player and Jack Nicklaus in the 1960s.

Between them they captured all the world's leading tournaments, and a great many of the other tournaments as well. But they also captured the public's imagination as golf suddenly became more popular with the masses. Arnold Palmer, as we have seen, played a very important role in that development but Player and Nicklaus also became favorites with golf fans as the sport grew in popularity in all corners of the globe.

As far as winning was concerned they seemed to have a monopoly on that. Between 1958 when Palmer won the Masters, and 1975 when Nicklaus won both the Masters and PGA title, they won 29 of the 72 major championships open to them and in only one year, 1969, did they fail to win at least one major between them. Between 1960 and 1966 no one else won the Masters title as the three held a seven year domination of the event.

Jack Nicklaus has been, by far, the most successful in terms of prize money and tournament wins. His record of 18 professional majors is seven better than the next man, Walter Hagen, who won 11 titles.

Nicklaus, nicknamed 'The Golden Bear', was born at Columbus, Ohio, in 1940 and was the US Amateur champion in 1959 and 1961. However, he really served notice that an outstanding talent was about to unfold when he pushed Palmer all the way in the 1960 Open at Cherry Hills before succumbing to Palmer's final round 65. He turned the tables at Oakmont in 1962 when he beat Arnie by three strokes in an 18-hole play-off to win the title. It was Jack's first win as a professional. What a way to start!

The following year he won the first of his record six Masters titles, and completed a double by capturing the first of his five PGA titles. Having won the Masters for a second time in 1965 he made it back-to-back victories the following year. No man has since retained his

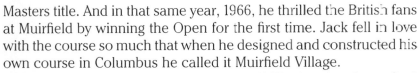

ABOVE: *Two thirds of 'The Big Three', Gary Player (right) and Jack Nicklaus shake hands after the South African had beaten the 'Golden Bear' 5 & 4 to retain his World Match Play title in 1966.*

LEFT: *It's all smiles for Kel Nagle (left) and Gary Player after they had tied the 1965 US Open. The following day it was Player who kept on smiling after his three stroke win.*

Masters title. And in that same year, 1966, he thrilled the British fans at Muirfield by winning the Open for the first time. Jack fell in love with the course so much that when he designed and constructed his own course in Columbus he called it Muirfield Village.

Nicklaus won his second US Open in 1967 when he shot a final round 65 to Palmer's 69 to beat Arnie by four strokes and established a new US Open record low score of 275, beating Ben Hogan's 1948 total by one. As the 1970s rolled in so Jack Nicklaus matured in golfing terms and the best from him was still to be seen.

RIGHT: *Arnold Palmer looking dejected during the 1966 US Open play-off with Billy Casper. He had every right to – he had thrown away a seven stroke lead the previous day and should never have been in the play-off.*

RIGHT: *A kiss and a smile says it all after Gary Player became the youngest winner of the Open since Young Tom Morris. Player was only 23 at the time of his 1959 success at Muirfield.*

BELOW: *A familiar Jack Nicklaus pose.*

By now an established member of the US Ryder Cup team, he won his second British Open at St Andrews in 1970 when he beat Doug Sanders by one stroke in an 18-hole play-off. He captured the PGA title in 1971 and had one of his finest years in 1972 when he won the Masters and the US Open at Pebble Beach. He was also second to Lee Trevino in the British Open at Muirfield.

By the mid-seventies the 'Triumvirate' was no longer as dominant as it had been but Nicklaus carried on winning. He won the PGA title three more times, in 1973, 1975 and 1980, the British Open on just one more occasion, at St Andrews in 1978 when he won by two strokes from the little known New Zealander Simon Owen, and fellow Americans Ben Crenshaw, Tom Kite and Ray Floyd. Two years later he won his only other US Open when he beat Japan's Isao Aoki into second place at Baltusrol. But Jack Nicklaus was to continue to be the Master of Augusta and he added title number five in 1975. Eleven years later, when many thought the Championship-winning days of Jack Nicklaus were over, he staged a remarkable comeback on the back nine to shoot a 65 for a 279 total and win from Greg Norman and Tom Kite. Jack was 46 years and 3 months old at the time. It was one of the sport's most remarkable wins.

Add to his amazing list of majors other great successes like six times winner of the Australian Open, member of six World Cup winning teams, winner of the World Match play title and member of six Ryder Cup teams and you will appreciate what an outstanding golfer Jack Nicklaus has been. His 71 US Tour wins are second only to Sam Snead's record of 84 and Jack, in 1988, became the first man to win over $5 million on the US Tour.

However, just because Jack was the most dominant of the trio, it doesn't mean the others played any lesser role in their contribution to the sport's popularity in the sixties and early seventies.

Arnold Palmer certainly did his share for both the golf fans and fellow professionals alike as we have seen. But he also enjoyed a successful playing career and was the first of the three men to win one of the majors when he won the Masters in 1958 and, at the age of 28, became the youngest winner since Byron Nelson in 1937. Having finished third in 1959 he regained the title the following year, after leading after each of the first three rounds. Despite this he found himself trailing Ken Venturi by one shot with two holes to play but two closing birdies were enough to give Palmer the title. Also in 1960 he had one of the most remarkable turnarounds to win a major championship when he reversed a seven stroke deficit at the end of 54 holes to win the US Open title by two strokes from the young amateur Jack Nicklaus. That same year he narrowly failed in his bid to win the Centenary British Open at the first attempt. But the following year he did win the British Open and at Troon in 1962 he retained the title.

Palmer had also won his third Masters title in 1962 and been beaten in a play-off by Jack Nicklaus in the US Open at Oakmont. He was also beaten in a play-off for the US Open the following year when Julius Boros beat him and Jack Cupit at Brookline's first Open since 1913.

Arnold Palmer won the Masters in 1964 by six strokes from Dave Marr and Jack Nicklaus. It was his fourth victory in the event in seven years, but sadly it was to be the last major for one of the greatest names in golf.

He finished joint second with Player behind Nicklaus in the 1965 Masters and in 1963 lost a play-off for the US Open title for a third time

LEFT: *Gary Player in his distinctive all-black outfit. Player is renowned to be one of the finest bunker players and spent hours practicing such shots in his early days.*

RIGHT: *Jack Nicklaus and Arnold Palmer (seen here during the 1987 Masters) always had that sense of fun but at the same time played the game seriously and competitively.*

BELOW: *The plaque on Royal Birkdale's old 15th fairway to commemorate a great shot by Arnold Palmer on his way to winning the 1961 Open.*

when he lost to Billy Casper. But, in contrast to his 1960 win, Palmer this time threw away a seven stroke lead and then lost the play-off the next day. How fortunes change in golf! Palmer also finished joint second in the PGA Championship in 1968 and 1970. It is the only major Palmer has not won, despite coming close three times.

But the contribution Arnold Palmer made to golf is not measured only in championship victories as we have already seen.

And so to the final member of golf's 'third Triumvirate,' the diminutive South African, Gary Player. Born at Johannesburg in 1935 he established himself in the 1960s as the finest non-American golfer in the world and was one of the few men capable of taking on, and beating, the Americans in their own backyard. His record of 21 wins on the US Tour is testament itself to his outstanding ability.

Having already established himself in his homeland as an outstanding golfer he showed the world his talents in 1959 when he shot a final round 68 to win the British Open at Muirfield. Having won on US soil in 1957 he captured the American public's hearts by becoming the first non-American winner of the Masters in 1961 when he beat Arnie Palmer and Charlie Coe into second place. The following year he won the PGA Championship and consequently had won three different majors in four years. There only remained the US Open to complete the set and that win came in 1965 when he became only the third man after Gene Sarazen and Ben Hogan to win all four majors. Jack Nicklaus became the fourth and last to date to achieve this feat with his British Open success the following year.

At Bellerive, Missouri, Player beat the Australian Kel Nagle by three strokes in an 18 hole play-off. He was the first non-American to win the title since Britain's Ted Ray in 1920. Over the next 13 years he was to win five more majors starting with the British Open over Carnoustie's monster course in 1968. In 1972 he won his second PGA title when he beat Tommy Aaron and Jim Jamieson at Oakland Hills and in 1974 Gary Player enjoyed his most successful year. He emerged at the front of the pack after a tight finish to win his second Masters title and at Lytham he beat Britain's Peter Oosterhuis by six strokes after emerging from a 71st hole scare when it looked as though he might have lost his ball. The only one black cloud on the horizon in 1974 was Player's 3 & 1 defeat by Hale Irwin in the final of the World Matchplay championship at Wentworth. It was Player's sixth final since the tournament was inaugurated in 1964 and was his first defeat. He was undoubtedly the matchplay 'king' at that time.

Player had been winning majors in three different decades and when he won his last title, the 1978 Masters, he was in his 43rd year. Nevertheless he defied his years to haul back a seven stroke defecit in the last round, including seven birdies over the tough last ten holes, to beat Hubert Green and Tom Watson.

Upon reaching his 50th birthday in 1985 Gary Player returned to winning ways on the US Seniors Tour where he joined Arnold Palmer. Nicklaus became eligible to join the Tour in January 1990 and what nostalgia it will bring if those three men tour together again regularly like they did in the sixties.

BRITAIN BACK IN THE LIMELIGHT

With the arrival of Nicklaus, Palmer and Player it meant the chance of Britain regaining supremacy in the world of golf was very slim. Not since 1951 when Max Faulkner won at Royal Portrush had a Briton won his own Open. And not since Ted Ray's win in the 1920 US Open at Inverness had a Briton won a major championship on American soil. As the 1960s came to a close the chance of a repeat victory in either tournament still seemed remote, but then along came the son of a Scunthorpe steelworker, Tony Jacklin.

Jacklin learned his trade under the watchful eye of Bill Shankland at Potters Bar. He turned professional at the age of 18 and two years later he was the winner of the prestigious Dunlop Masters title. That was in 1967. The following year he set off for America where he was convinced he could win among the best golfers in the world. Furthermore he knew that if he was to be regarded one day as a true great of the game he had to win on US soil.

Jacklin's first US victory soon came when he captured the Jacksonville Open, but he had a lot more in store for the British fans who had been starved of success for so long. Four hundred and twenty-four hopefuls entered the 1969 British Open which was to be played over the links of the Royal Lytham and St Annes club on the northwest English coast. Among the field who gathered at Lytham was a strong American contingent including Nicklaus, Miller Barber, Gay Brewer, Orville Moody, Bert Yancey and Billy Casper. But in the event they were held in little regard by the rest of the field and the first five places were filled by non-Americans.

The Australian Peter Thomson and Argentina's Roberto de Vicenzo both came within a whisker of regaining the title and Christy O'Connor was four shots off the lead on 284. But pride of place went to Scunthorpe's favorite son whose four rounds of 68, 70, 70 and 72 were enough to secure victory by two shots from the left-handed New Zealander, Bob Charles.

As Jacklin walked up the final fairway the noise from the partisan British crowd was deafening. It had been 18 years since they had seen one of their own golfers walk up to the 72nd hole with the title in his grasp.

Tony Jacklin's victory did more than ensure Britain's first champion since 1951. He was an inspiration for so many people, young and old to take up the great game. Many people identified themselves with Jacklin's background and thought they could emulate his performance. Most, of course, stood little or no chance of making the grade in the world of professional golf. But some did, and the strength in depth of the British game today stems from Jacklin's great day at Lytham in 1969. And it didn't end there.

ABOVE RIGHT: *Tony Jacklin was the first Briton since 1920 to win on the US Tour when he captured the 1968 Greater Jacksonville Open. It was to herald a marvelous two year spell for Jacklin, who later became the skipper of the European Ryder Cup team. He won the British Open in 1969 and in 1970 led from the front to win the US Open.*

RIGHT: *A smiling Dave Hill, runner-up to Jacklin in the 1970 US Open at Hazeltine. Hill had some scathing remarks to make about the course including; 'A monkey could play this course as well as a man'; 'sheep were being robbed of good grazing land'; and 'All the course needs is 80 acres of corn and four cows'. In the round following those latter remarks, Hill was greeted with 'moos' from the gallery following his match!*

LEFT: *Tony Jacklin works on the practice ground on his way to his memorable British Open win at Lytham in 1969.*

TOP: *A kiss for Jacklin from his wife Vivien after capturing the US Open. Sadly for Jacklin and his three children, Vivien tragically died near their Spanish home in 1988.*

ABOVE: *Not far behind Tony Jacklin at Lytham in 1969 was Christy O'Connor Snr., one of the finest players to come out of Ireland.*

RIGHT: *It's all over and Jacklin is Britain's first champion since Max Faulkner in 1951.*

BELOW: *Two men tied for third place, just one stroke behind runner-up Bob Charles, in the 1969 British Open at Lytham. One of them was the 1967 champion Roberto de Vicenzo of Argentina.*

BOTTOM: *Billy Casper was one of the Americans who made the trip to Lytham in 1969. After two good opening rounds of 70 he faded away and ended 13 shots off the lead.*

A year later he emulated Ted Ray and won the US Open. Moreover, his victory was one of the most convincing in the history of the tournament. Jacklin led from start to finish and ended up seven shots ahead of second placed Dave Hill. It was the biggest winning margin since Jim Barnes won by nine shots from Walter Hagen and Fred McLeod at Columbia, Maryland, in 1921. Jacklin established himself as a true world class golfer that day at the monster Hazeltine course in Minnesota. The following year he confirmed his arrival among golf's elite when he regained his Jacksonville Open title.

Since then Tony Jacklin has done much for golf in Britain. He has served as the captain of the PGA and has of course been the man who has led Europe to memorable Ryder Cup wins over the United States.

Walter Hagen did so much for the game of professional golf in the 1920s. So did Arnold Palmer forty years later. But in Britain the man who put British golf on the map, and helped keep it there, was Tony Jacklin.

SUDDENLY IT'S A YOUNG MAN'S GAME

With the domination of Nicklaus and co. coming to an end, the door was open for a flood of youngsters, who had all dreamed of emulating their heroes, to burst on to the golfing scene. And how they arrived!

Suddenly golf was no longer regarded as a sport for the wealthy. It was a game open to everybody. Ordinary people took to the sport in their hundreds of thousands. The laws of probability dictated that such vast numbers must produce champions and they came along in the shape of Tom Watson, Johnny Miller and so on.

The winners of the majors had traditionally been, more often than not, in their thirties. But in the mid 1970s it was commonplace for players in their twenties to win titles and today the age of winners is

coming down all the time as players like Jose-Maria Olazabal, the talented Spaniard, have shown.

As the 1970s arrived Dave Stockton, at 28 years of age, won the PGA Championship. A third round 66 clinched the title for him as he left Bob Murphy and Arnold Palmer trailing by two shots in second place. That was to set the pace for much of the seventies with new young faces at the top of leaderboards, with the established names in their wake.

The first of the real stars to emerge as a challenger to the established golfers of the 1960s was San Franciscan Johnny Miller. As a 19-year-old amateur in 1966 he finished eighth in the US Open over his home course at the Olympic Club. He was resigned to acting as a caddie but surprised himself by qualifying for the tournament. He was to turn out to be the golden boy of the 70s and 'arrived' when he shot a final round 63 to win the Open at Oakmont in 1973. That was to herald the start of three great seasons for Miller. The following year he dominated golf in the United States and in successive weeks won the Phoenix Open and Tucson Open with scores of 24 and 25 under par respectively. Scoring like that had never been seen on the US Tour before. In each tournament he shot a round of 61. Although he didn't win a major in 1974 he won the Tournament of Champions and World Open, and displaced Jack Nicklaus at the top of the US money

LEFT: *Johnny Miller emerged as a real threat to Jack Nicklaus in the 1970s and he confirmed his ability when he won the 1973 US Open title at Oakmont. He was only 26 at the time.*

RIGHT: *Although he had been on the US Tour since 1964, it was not until after winning the 1975 US Open that Lou Graham received international attention.*

BELOW: *John Mahaffey (right) was one of the new breed of younger professionals to emerge in the 1970s. He is seen here enjoying a joke with Lou Graham before the two engaged in a play-off for the 1975 US Open which Graham won by two shots.*

list. By 1976 the career of Johnny Miller was on the decline but the slide was temporarily halted with success in the British Open at Royal Birkdale.

Second to Miller that day was the seasoned Jack Nicklaus and another youngster, who has since gone on to become one of the biggest names in world golf, Severiano Ballesteros. Seve was a brash youngster of 19 when he appeared at Birkdale. But he showed great composure and skill to threaten the 'master', Jack Nicklaus, and the young pretender, Johnny Miller, with two opening rounds of 69. Although he was six strokes behind Miller at the end of four rounds, Seve's day was to come and in 1979, at the age of 24, he captured the British Open for the first time. A Lytham course-record 65 in the second round helped him secure a three stroke win from the strong American pairing of Nicklaus and Ben Crenshaw, another fresh face to arrive on the scene.

From the moment he arrived in the world of professional golf Severiano Ballesteros served notice that he would one day be a champion, and a champion he has been. He has won the British Open three times, the Masters twice, and has enjoyed success on the US Tour as well as in other leading golfing centers around the world. Although he only passed 30 in 1987, he is now regarded as one of the game's senior players. But even Ballesteros has to be on his guard because the new breed of 'pretenders' is getting younger all the time.

While the challenge of Johnny Miller to Jack Nicklaus' crown faltered after a promising start, the next youngster to come along and threaten the 'Golden Bear' was Tom Watson. He won the first of five British Open titles at Carnoustie in 1975 at the age of 25 when he beat Jack Newton in a play-off. A psychology graduate from Stanford University, Watson had won the first of his 32 US Tour events in 1974 when he captured the Western Open. By 1977 he had added the Masters title to his list of honors and also topped US money list.

Watson took his winning into the eighties and he took over as number one from Nicklaus. In 1989 he surpassed Jack's all-time

career winnings total and enjoyed a revival in his fortunes when he was recalled to play in the US Ryder Cup team shortly after his 40th birthday.

Other youngsters also emerged in the 1970s and enjoyed their moment of glory. Hale Irwin and Andy North both won the US Open while still in their 20s and when Jerry Pate won by two shots from Al Geiberger and Tom Weiskopf in 1976 he was only 22 years of age. Lanny Wadkins and Fuzzy Zoeller both added their names to the major honors board in the seventies, again while in their twenties, to confirm it was very much a young man's game.

But the arrival of youngsters was not just restricted to those who became immediate champions. There were others like Bill Rogers, Craig Stadler, Ben Crenshaw and Tom Kite. In Britain youngsters like Sandy Lyle and Nick Faldo were coming through the amateur ranks. These men all eventually made their mark on world golf as the new breed took over from the established names. No longer did any one player have a domination on world golf. Suddenly there were too many top class players for that. And because of that the 1980s became one of golf's finest eras.

Jack Nicklaus had little regard for its severity as they set the tone with two opening rounds of 68. After that they matched each other's scores until the fourth round.

Although Watson and Nicklaus both shot level par, 70, in the second round, the day belonged to a fellow American, Mark Hayes, who shot an Open record 63 with an outward 32 and an inward 31. But the remainder of the championship belonged to Nicklaus and Watson.

They both carded 65s in the third round and after three and a half rounds Nicklaus had a one stroke lead. He was two up after the 12th hole on the final round. Three holes later they were all square with three to play. They both had level par 4s at the 16th but then Nicklaus took a 5 to Watson's 4 at the 17th and that proved decisive. They both birdied the 18th and Watson ran out the winner by just one stroke after 72 holes of record-breaking golf.

In addition to Hayes' record 18-hole total, Watson's four-round total of 268 beat the Open record by a staggering eight strokes (Nicklaus' total was seven better than the old record), and is still a championship record more than 12 years later. Watson's score over the last 36 was also a Championship record as was his last 54-hole total. There were 40 rounds under 70 and it cannot be denied that the course was playing easier than most others used for the Open. But the big problem facing the rest of the field was in playing consistent golf. Watson and Nicklaus did just that, and proof lies in the fact that Hubert Green in third place was 11 shots behind the winner.

Although beaten at Turnberry, Jack Nicklaus had two years earlier been the victor in what has been described as 'The Greatest Masters of Them All'. Nicklaus has been involved in some great finishes but none has been finer than on that April day in 1975 when he was involved in a classic with Johnny Miller and Tom Weiskopf.

Miller had emerged in the mid-seventies as the man most likely to topple Nicklaus. He had won seven Tour events in 1974 and headed the money list. He was certainly Nicklaus' biggest rival. But from nowhere appeared Weiskopf, hoping to end his sequence of three runner-up positions in the Masters and eventually capture the elusive green jacket.

ABOVE RIGHT: *There was a lot of elation around the 18th green at Augusta in 1975 as Weiskopf birdied to take a one stroke lead over Nicklaus at the end of the third round.*

RIGHT: *Mr and Mrs Watson enjoy Tom's first British Open success at Carnoustie in 1975 after he beat the unlucky Australian Jack Newton in an 18 hole play-off.*

LEFT: *Doug Sanders came agonisingly close to winning the 1970 Open at St Andrews. Needing to two putt the 72nd hole to win the title he took three putts, then lost a play-off with Jack Nicklaus.*

ABOVE: *Lee Trevino engaged in one of the most intriguing battles in British Open history at Birkdale in 1971 before he eventually won by one stroke from Taiwan's 'Mr Lu'.*

Nicklaus went round with amateur Curtis Strange on the first day and shot a 68, just one off the surprise leader Bobby Nichols. Eighteen holes later Nicklaus led the field by five strokes after a 67 to give a two round total of 135. Weiskopf was on 141 and Miller on 146. Little did the Augusta fans realise but the responsibility for trying to prevent the 'Golden Bear' from winning his fifth Masters title would, two days later, rest on the shoulders of these two men as they were to engage in a nail-biting finish on the 72nd green.

Surprisingly Nicklaus lost his lead in the third round after shooting a 73 to Weiskopf's 66. Miller carded a third round 65 and had moved into third place but was three behind Nicklaus. Going into the last 18 holes the scores read: Weiskopf 207, Nicklaus 208, Miller 211. But what fireworks there were to come.

Hale Irwin set the pace by equalling the Masters' record with a 64 and low scoring was to be a major feature of the final day's play. Nicklaus and Weiskopf exchanged the lead three times. Approaching the 16th the two men were level, with Miller one behind. But then Nicklaus delivered one of those 'killer' blows which he has done so often in the past. He holed a monster 40-foot putt for a birdie. He was one up and completed his round in 68 for a four-round total 276. He was playing ahead of Weiskopf and Miller, who were playing together. They came to the 18th green both knowing that they had to make a birdie to force a play-off with Nicklaus.

Miller had a 20-footer for his birdie whereas Weiskopf's putt was considerably easier, from 8 feet. Miller missed and lost his chance. And then, to his horror, Weiskopf watched as his putt, which was on line, suddenly stopped short and suddenly his chance of winning his first Masters title also disappeared. As for Nicklaus, he confirmed once more that he was the Master of Augusta and won his fifth title in one of the most gripping finishes to a major tournament in the 1970s.

THE EUROPEANS

When Severiano Ballesteros finished runner-up in the Open at Royal Birkdale in 1976 he showed that he was a champion in the making. Jack Nicklaus who shared second place with him that day, predicted the young Spaniard would go on to win many championships.

Jack has, of course, been proved right. But not only has Ballesteros opened the door for other Spanish golfers, he has been the inspiration to golfers on the continent of Europe who have made a big impression on the golf world in the 1980s.

The son of a farmer from Santander in Northern Spain, Ballesteros was a scratch golfer at the age of 12, following his brothers Manuel, Baldomero and Vicente who were all top class players. He joined the European Tour in 1974 and in 1976 enjoyed his first Tour success in

RIGHT: *Spaniard Severiano Ballesteros has not only emerged as one of Europe's outstanding golfers in the past 15 years, but also one of the world's top players and has frequently taken on and beaten the Americans on their home soil.*

LEFT: *West Germany's Bernhard Langer acknowledges the applause of the large Augusta crowd on his way to winning the Masters in 1985.*

ABOVE: *Bernhard Langer and Seve Ballesteros vied for the number one position in Europe for a couple of seasons but then the German sadly got hit by the dreaded 'yips' which seriously affected his game.*

the Dutch Open. At Birkdale he blasted two opening rounds of 69 as he showed little regard for the famous course or his more illustrious rivals who were challenging for the British Open. Although he fell away with a final day 74 he showed his true potential. And that great potential has now been realised.

He captured his first major championship in 1979 when he won the British Open at Lytham, thanks largely to a course record 65 in the second round, but the big breakthrough came at Augusta nine months later when, at the age of 23, he became the youngest winner of the Masters. Seve had already won on the US Tour when he captured the 1978 Greater Greensboro Open and the American golf fans were not surprised when he became the first non-American winner of the Masters since Gary Player.

He won the Masters again in 1983 when he had a resounding four stroke win from Ben Crenshaw and Tom Kite. Suddenly, it seemed that the Americans were vulnerable in the big events, as well as in their own domestic competitions. Ballesteros was to prove to be a regular visitor, and winner, on American soil.

Ballesteros won his second British Open at St Andrews in 1984, and in 1986 he became the first man to gross career earnings of £1 million in Europe. Two years later he won the British Open a third time when he captured the title, once more at Lytham. Seve had well and truly opened a door for European golf and in the early eighties he was joined at the top by Bernhard Langer of West Germany. Between them they became the scourge of American golfers.

Langer's road to the top was longer and harder than Seve's. He had turned professional in 1972 but had to wait until 1980 for his first

ABOVE: *Sweden has produced some good class golfers in the 1980s, Anders Forsbrand probably being the best of them. In 1987 he became the first Swede to win a strokeplay event on the European Tour and narrowly missed Ryder Cup selection.*

LEFT: *Spain has emerged as one of Europe's top golfing nations in the last decade and their senior player is Jose Maria Canizares, a Tour member since 1971.*

LEFT: *Another Spaniard, Manuel Pinero, has also been on the Tour since 1971.*

RIGHT: *The excellent line of Spanish golfers has been maintained with the arrival of Jose Maria Olazabal. In 1985 he was the British Youths champion. The following season he was second on the European money list with over £155,000. Twelve months later he was a member of the European Ryder Cup team which won the Cup on US soil for the first time. And who will ever forget his rendition of the* La Bamba *dance to celebrate the occasion.*

European Tour success when he won the Dunlop Masters. The following year he was runner-up to Bill Rogers in the British Open at Sandwich and that same year was the top-money winner in Europe. However, the dreaded 'yips', which had crept into his game in 1976, re-appeared in 1982. But he overcame them and finished second again in the British Open. This time he was beaten by Ballesteros at St Andrews in 1984. The following year Langer confirmed a great revival in European golf fortunes when he won the US Masters and Sea Pines Classic in successive weeks; a rare feat on the US Tour.

Langer and Ballesteros became deadly rivals as they vied for the honor of 'Top European Golfer' but they also teamed up in the European Ryder Cup teams where they became vital members of Tony Jacklin's winning combinations.

European golf has enjoyed its greatest ever period in the 1980s and a lot of the credit goes to the talents and exploits of Seve Ballesteros. Consequently many youngsters have emerged to help continue the long line of potential champions to come from the Continent.

Seve was unquestionably the inspiration for the latest Spanish golden boy of golf, Jose-Maria Olazabal. But other countries are making advances. One such country is Sweden which has produced winners on the European Tour. Mats Lanner became his country's first winner when he captured the Epson Grand Prix in 1987 and since then Anders Forsbrand and Ove Sellberg have added their names to the European 'Roll of Champions.' Magnus Persson is another talented Swede who is threatening to make the big breakthrough in the near future.

France is also starting to produce some fine players and in 1989 they sprung one of the big shocks of the 80s when they knocked one of the fancied teams, Australia, out of the Dunhill Cup at St Andrews.

The last three US Ryder Cup captains; Lee Trevino, Jack Nicklaus and Raymond Floyd don't need reminding about the strength of European golf in the 1980s. With so many talented youngsters on the fringe of success, it looks as though life is going to be tough for the Americans for a few years to come.

EUROPE IN THE RYDER CUP
THE END OF US DOMINATION

When professional golfers from Britain and the United States first did battle for the Ryder Cup in 1927 the Americans had a very convincing win on home soil. When the fourth match was completed in 1933 both teams had each won two matches. That was to be the end of British glory until 1957 when they won at Lindrick and that win was an isolated moment of joy for the British fans.

When the United States notched up their 18th win (to Britain's three) at Royal Lytham in 1977, the matches were becoming such one-sided affairs that in boxing parlance they would have been described as 'No Contest.'

Something had to be done to revive interest in a declining tournament. At Greenbrier, West Virginia, in 1979, the British team recruited help from the Spaniards Antonio Garrido and Seve Ballesteros. The name of the team was changed to that of Europe. John Jacobs had the honor of leading the first European team and despite trailing 5½-2½ at the end of the first day did well to come back on day two

LEFT: *The hero of the 1985 Ryder Cup, Scotland's Sam Torrance who clinched the match for Europe and thus inflicted the first defeat in 28 years on the Americans.*

RIGHT: *After a poor start in the 1985 Ryder Cup, when he lost his opening foursomes, Bernhard Langer was unbeaten in his other four matches and in the singles had a 5 & 4 win over Hal Stutton.*

ABOVE: *Larry Nelson was recalled for Ryder Cup duties in 1987 after a six year lay off, but he was powerless to prevent a first European win on US soil. He didn't win any of his four matches.*

PREVIOUS PAGE: *Sam Torrance playing out of water at the 12th during the 1985 Ryder Cup at The Belfry.*

LEFT: *One of the most outstanding players in world golf in 1987 was Ian Woosnam and he crowned a memorable year by playing on the winning Ryder Cup team.*

RIGHT: *Seve Ballesteros sinks his putt to seal the European victory at Muirfield Village in 1987.*

and trail by just one point. Sadly the new European team was let down in the singles just as the Great Britain team had been over the years.

The Americans came away from Greenbrier with another fairly convincing 17-11 win and once more kept possession of the Ryder Cup. Little did they know at the time that the foundation stone had been laid upon which European success was to be built within the next ten years. Mind you, the Europeans' performance at Walton Heath two years later gave little indication that glory was just around the corner.

There was no Ballesteros in 1981 but the European contingent in the new format team was up to three. Spaniards Manuel Pinero and Jose-Maria Canizares were joined by German Bernhard Langer. The opening day saw the European team, again led by Jacobs, enjoy a rare lead, at 4½ points to 3½. Then it went all wrong on day two with the Americans winning seven of the eight matches.

So, after two attempts the new European team had failed to wrest the trophy from the Americans. Further action was needed and that action involved the recruiting of a new captain. The next man to lead the challenge was Tony Jacklin.

He so nearly gained instant success when he took his gallant team to Palm Beach Gardens in 1983. Again they led by one point at the end of the first day. But the second day was a different story this time. No longer were the Europeans intimidated by their American counterparts and going into the singles the match was finely poised at 8-all.

Nick Faldo, Bernhard Langer, Paul Way and Ken Brown all claimed notable scalps on the final day but in the end it was not quite enough and the Americans won by a single point. It was the closest the United States had come to defeat since the tied match at Royal Birkdale in 1969. Two years later Tony Jacklin's men did what they had come close to doing in Florida when they won the Cup for the first time in 28 years. It was a memorable performance by the likes of Paul Way, Howard Clark, Ballesteros, Faldo and so on as they clinched the cup with Sam Torrance's remarkable and emotional win over Andy North in the singles. It crowned a great career for Tony Jacklin and gave him as much, if not more, satisfaction than when he won the British and US Open titles 15 years earlier.

The strength of European golf was now being truly appreciated and America was being bombarded with an influx of top quality European players ready to make an impact on the US Tour. Apart from Langer and Ballesteros, Ken Brown, Nick Faldo and Sandy Lyle all enjoyed success on the US Tour.

The next goal for Tony Jacklin and his band of warriors was to win the Ryder Cup in America. That feat had never been achieved before. Could they bring off a remarkable win at Muirfield Village in 1987? Nicklaus was the American captain for the match, to be played over a course he had designed and named after the venue of his first British Open success. Jacklin still had charge of the European team and they arrived in the States with confidence sky-high. US golfing pride had taken a severe dent at the Belfry two years earlier. They desperately needed to restore it at Muirfield Village.

How the Europeans rubbed it home on the first day to finish leading by 6 matches to 2. The heroes of Europe's first day were the Spanish pairing of Ballesteros and his young 'pretender' Jose-Maria Olazabal. They won their foursomes and fourballs and the next morning carried on where they left off as Europe raced to an 8½-3½ point lead. Going into the singles they still led by five points and when Ballesteros beat Curtis Strange the Americans had lost on home soil for the first time in the Cup's 60 year history. But the European success did not lie only in the performance of its established stars like Ballesteros and Langer. Men like Eamonn Darcy, Gordon Brand junior and Jose Rivero all played a crucial role in a team welded together by Tony Jacklin.

The Ryder Cup became a big attraction once more and there is no doubting that the addition of European golfers to the event helped its popularity. Their presence certainly prevented it from being the constant 'No Contest' which it had become. It has now rightly been restored to its place as one of the world's great international sporting contests.

THE OTHER TOURS

Tournament golf at the highest professional level is not just restricted to the US and European Tours. Golf is played worldwide and consequently the professional game has become more organised in the last fifteen years or so. The forerunner of the current US Tour dates to the 1920s, while the European PGA Tour has been in existence since 1975. But what about the other professional golf Tours?

One Tour that has definitely grown in popularity in recent years is the US Senior Tour which is open to professionals over the age of 50. Because of the influx of some great names like Arnold Palmer and Gary Player in recent years, the Tour has become a great attraction with the golf fans as these great players take their skills around the United States for more than 30 tournaments each year. Big money has been brought into the Seniors game and most of the players are now playing for, and winning, much more money than they ever did in their regular Tour days.

One of the biggest Tours outside the United States in terms of prizemoney is the Asian Tour. It started life as the Far East Tour in 1959 when Australian professional Eric Cremin and Welshman Kim Hall organised the Hong Kong Open. This was the foundation for the Tour which really started in 1961 with the Philippines, Hong Kong and Singapore Opens forming the basis of the Tour. The Asian Golf Confederation was founded in 1963 and since then the Thailand, Indonesia, Japanese, Korean, Taiwan, Indian and Malaysian Opens, have all formed rounds on the Tour. The organisation was renamed the Asia Golf Circuit in the 1970s and by the end of the decade big name sponsors were lending their names, and money, to the top tournaments. In 1977 the Tour had its first $100,000 tournament, in Tokyo.

Today ten tournaments make up the Asian Tour, but out of the Tour was spawned the Japanese Tour consisting of more than 30

RIGHT: *Fiji's Vijay Singh, who won the Volvo Open on the European Tour in 1989.*

BELOW: *The Arab States are certainly a potential growth area for all sports, including golf. Mark James has already been there and won as can be seen by this amazing trophy being presented to him by the racehorse owner Sheikh Mohammed.*

LEFT: *The Japanese Tour has developed some fine players in recent years. Tommy Nakajima has been a professional since 1975 and a regular member of the US Tour since 1983. Although he has not won on Tour he has been a consistent money winner. However, he won't need reminding of his dreadful three month spell back in 1978 when, first, he took 13 shots at the 13th at Augusta in the Masters. And then, three months later, he took nine at St Andrews' infamous Road Hole after being up among the leaders.*

RIGHT: *Golf has become increasingly popular in Japan in recent years. Consequently she has produced more star players, like 'Jumbo' Ozaki.*

BELOW: *Another fine Japanese player is Isao Aoki who has played on the US Tour since 1981. He was the winner of the 1978 World Match Play title at Wentworth.*

ABOVE: *The US Seniors Tour has grown rapidly in recent years and is very popular. Men like Billy Casper (pictured) are earning more money from the Tour than they were in their regular Tour days. Jack Nicklaus was eligible for entry in 1990 and joined his two former foes, Gary Player and Arnold Palmer, to add even more interest to Seniors golf.*

LEFT: *The Australian golf circuit has constantly thrown up some excellent golfers. In recent years Greg Norman has been the most outstanding.*

RIGHT: *The 'Great White Shark' in full flow.*

BOTTOM, FAR LEFT: *Prior to the arrival of Greg Norman, Australia's leading player was David Graham, who has now made a home for himself in the United States and has been a prominent member of the US Tour since 1971. He was the PGA Champion in 1973 and US Open champion two years later.*

BELOW LEFT: *Now enjoying his golf as a Senior, Arnold Palmer won more money from the Seniors Skins Game in January 1990 than he ever did in a full season on the regular Tour, and he spent 30 years on the regular Tour!*

events with names like the Chunichi Crowns Tournament, Yomiuri Sapporo and NST Niigata Open, which all indicate the heavy involvement of sponsorship.

Because of the increase in popularity among the Asian countries, some fine golfers have emerged from the Orient. Firstly there was the diminutive 'Mr Lu' – Lu Liang Huan, from Taiwan and then came along some notable Japanese golfers like Isao Aoki, Jumbo Ozaki and Tommy Nakajima. Another Taiwan golfer, T. C. Chen, has emerged from the Asian Tour to become a regular competitor on the US Tour, highlighting what an excellent breeding ground Asia is for golfers . . . but so is Australia . . .

The Australian Tour is held during the European and American winter months which, of course, is summertime 'Down Under.' It gives the opportunity for top golfers to play golf at the highest level twelve months of the year if they so desire. Many, however, use winter time as a period for relaxation and gathering their thoughts for the forthcoming season. Nonetheless the Australian Tour continues to attract big names, notably to their leading tournaments like the Australian Open, New Zealand Open and Australian Masters. The Tour has also been a breeding ground for home-grown talent and in the latter part of the 1980s Australian golfers have made the transition from playing on home soil to the great golfing grounds of Europe and America with ease.

Peter Thomson was the first great Australasian in the 1950s and he was followed by the left-handed New Zealander Bob Charles. But in recent years Australia's David Graham has become a popular player, not to mention a regular winner, on the US Tour. He has been followed by the 'Great White Shark', Greg Norman, who has been the most popular and successful Australian in recent years.

Norman has come close so many times to winning more major honors than his solitary British Open success. He has established himself as a big money-winner on both sides of the Atlantic after first learning his trade on the Australian circuit.

Rodger Davis, Wayne Grady and Ian Baker-Finch have all carried on the fine tradition of Australian golfers and in the last couple of

years new names have emerged as Craig Parry and Mike Harwood have both become winners on the European Tour. New Zealand too has a rising newcomer in Fran Nobilo.

Africa is also a hot-bed of professional golf and their exists a South African Tour and a Safari Tour. The latter was often used by many of the lower ranked players in Europe as a pre-season warm-up before the start of the European Tour. In 1989 the Tour was split into an early- and then late-season Tour starting before the European Tour and concluding after the end of the European 'season.'

The five events which make up the Safari Tour are the Nigerian, Ivory Coast, 555 Kenya, Zimbabwe and Zambian Open Championships. The man who headed the money list in 1988 was Fiji's Vijay Singh who was a first-time winner on the European Tour in 1989. Others like Gordon J Brand, Bill Longmuir, Brian Waites and David Jagger have all been big money winners on the Safari Tour while never quite establishing themselves on the European Tour. The first Safari Tour event was the Kenya Open in 1967 which was won by Britain's Guy Wolstenholme.

Because of the increase in popularity of golf in South Africa, and thanks to the success of, firstly, Bobby Locke and then Gary Player, there has been a regular string of top golfers emerge from the South African Tour able to beat the Europeans and Americans.

Playing regularly on the US Tour at present are South Africans Fulton Allem, David Frost and Nick Price, while Zimbabwe's Denis Watson has enjoyed three US Tour wins and was fourth on the money list in 1984. Another Zimbabwean, Mark McNulty, has been a regular winner on the European Tour.

The structure of world golf permits real talent to come through and make it to the top and whether they start on the Safari, Japanese, Australian or Asian Tours, there is a chance that, because of their skills, they can emerge as a world champion. The ultimate of every golfer is to win a major championship. Many men have come from the Tours mentioned to do just that. Just because the four majors are played in the United States and Britain it does not mean that golf in the rest of the world is forgotten or second rate. It most certainly is not.

LET'S NOT FORGET THE LADIES

Women too enjoy the benefits of Tour golf, but largely in the United States and Britain.

Prizemoney in the ladies game in America is such that some leading tournaments, like the Dinah Shore and Nestlé World Championship, offer better first prizes than some events on the men's Tour. The leading US lady professionals can win in excess of $250,000 in a season, and in 1988 the top eight on the money list all surpassed that figure.

The Women's Professional Golf Association (WPGA) was formed in 1944 by three little-known lady golfers; Betty Hicks, Ellen Griffin, and Hope Seignious. After a couple of uncertain years the Wilson sports goods company came to their rescue and the Association was renamed the Ladies Professional Golf Association. Their marketing director was Fred Corcoran, Babe Zaharias' personal manager. From then on, the Association's fortunes took an upward turn, as did those of ladies golf in the United States.

By the end of 1950 a Tour had gained the support of golfers and spectators alike and in 1952 the number of tournaments had increased threefold to 21 events within a space of two years. Players of the day like Zaharias, Betsy Rawls, Peggy Kirk, and Louise Suggs all played a big role in the development of the ladies game.

By 1959 the total prizemoney on the Tour was up to $200,000 and in the early 1960s a fresh new face, Mickey Wright, joined the professional ranks. She became one of the dominant members of the Tour between 1961-64. Because of her exploits she gained media attention and suddenly the 'outside world' as Judy Rankin called it, took a second look at ladies golf, and liked what they saw. Once again there was an upsurge in popularity.

Television cameras rolled for the first time at an LPGA event in 1963, when the final round of the US Women's Open was covered. That was to start a long relationship between the television companies and ladies golf in America.

By the end of the 1960s total prizemoney had tripled to $600,000 and the girls were competing in 34 events each year. As the mid 70s arrived the Tour had expanded to an alarming degree and the LPGA struggled to keep up with the pace and in 1973 had to be rescued from the verge of bankruptcy.

In 1975 they recruited the services of Ray Volpe as their first Commissioner. He set about restructuring the Association. He recruited more staff and went in search of more corporate involvement. He

ABOVE: *Britain's Laura Davies took the US scene by storm in 1987 when she captured the US Women's Open in only her third season as a professional.*

LEFT: *One of the biggest money winners in ladies golf, Pat Bradley who has won well over $2½ million.*

FAR LEFT: *Jan Stephenson has had several offers to give up golf and take up modelling. It's plain to see why . . .*

was successful. In his seven years at the Association prizemoney went up from $1.5 million to $6.4 million with average purses increasing from $50,000 to $176,000. The number of professionals also increased and suddenly the number of entrants per tournament was up from 60 to 120. Television coverage was also increased from two to 14 tournaments a year. Under Volpe's successor, John D Laupheimer, the Tour continued to grow and annual purses are now in excess of $12 million and the number of women who have become golfing millionaires is rising every season.

Ladies golf in the United States is now firmly established and comes a close second in popularity to the men's Tour, along with the Senior Tour. The golfing public enjoys good quality golf, it does not matter whether it comes from Curtis Strange or Betsy King, so long as it is good.

ABOVE: *Kathy Whitworth turned professional in 1958 and has won more events than any other woman in history. Her total of 88 on the Women's Tour is four more than the men's 'champion' Sam Snead. Like Snead, strangely, she has never won the US Open.*

RIGHT: *One of the most successful women golfers in the last ten years has been Nancy Lopez. She turned professional in 1977 and in her rookie season won a staggering nine tournaments, including five in a row.*

ABOVE: *It took Betsy King seven years of trying before she eventually had her first success on the women's Tour. But since capturing the 1984 Kemper Open she has been a big winner on the Tour.*

RIGHT: *'Big Momma', Joanne Carner – the darling of the US fans for more than 30 years.*

The lady golfers of Britain and Europe have their own Tour, the WPG European Tour. Although prizemoney is considerably lower than that on offer to their American counterparts, the top money-winner can expect to bank winnings in six figures each year. The smaller size of the winnings does not detract from the intensity of competition among the girls from Britain and across Europe.

The Tour was taken over by the PGA in 1982, when a mere 30 or so players could be mustered up to take part in the tournaments. Now, because of the increased standard and popularity the Association has to be selective in its choice of new members. In the early eighties the WGA was only too pleased to welcome new members.

Because of the Tour, Britain has produced an outstanding champion in Laura Davies who surprised the Americans by winning the US Open after a play-off in 1987. Sweden's Liselotte Neumann and Spain's Marta Figueras-Dotti have both progressed from the European Tour to the US Tour and made their mark in America. Maria-Laure de Lorenzi de Taya is another talented European girl who is capable of beating the Americans on their home soil.

Women's golf has been played competitively for one hundred years. For so long it took a back seat to the man's game. Today it has a significant role in world golf.

161

THE STRENGTH IN DEPTH OF THE US TOUR

As we have already said, golf is no longer dominated by one or two men. Long gone are the days when Harry Vardon, Bobby Jones, Ben Hogan or Jack Nicklaus started the tournament as clear favorite. Golf is far more open these days. The days of one player being a 'brilliant driver' and another being a 'great short iron player' are also long gone. To survive in the world of professional golf in the 1980s, and 1990s, you have to be able to play every type of golf shot, with great consistency. Above all it is said that golf tournaments are won and lost on the putting surface.

We constantly see new names emerge at the top of leaderboards. Almost invariably the new names are American-bred talent, confirming what a successful 'production line' the golf 'factory' in the

ABOVE: *Curtis Strange holds aloft the US Open trophy after becoming the first man since Ben Hogan successfully to defend the title. Strange is on target to become the biggest money winner in golf history.*

RIGHT: *Lanny Wadkins has been one of the most consistent golfers on the US Tour in the last 20 years although he has not attracted the media attention of some of the other players.*

OPPOSITE PAGE: *The old breed and the new breed, Raymond Floyd (left) and Payne Stewart (right).*

RIGHT: *Unquestionably the man of the eighties on the US Tour was Curtis Northrup Strange.*

FAR RIGHT: *Fuzzy Zoeller has been a popular, and successful, member of the Tour for 15 years.*

BELOW: *Larry Nelson has quietly gone about his business during his 16 years on the Tour. He has won two PGA titles and one Open title, as well as pocketing over $3 million.*

United States has. During the 1980s 25 different men won majors and of those 25, no fewer than 19 were American . . . so what's all this talk of Europeans to the fore?

The established names were still around. Watson won five majors and Nicklaus and Larry Nelson won three each. Raymond Floyd won two titles in the 1980s and so did the new Golden Boy of US golf, Curtis Strange.

Strange won back-to-back US Open titles in 1988 and 1989, something not achieved since Ben Hogan in 1950-51. Since joining the Tour in 1977 he has emerged in the last five years as the biggest money winner. He was the first man to win $1 million in one season and has three times topped the money list. He will probably surpass Tom Watson's career winnings total during the 1990 season. A brash youngster when he first came on Tour, Strange has now settled down to become one of the finest, and most feared golfers in the world and his ability to keep on winning with such regularity, when there is so much talent waiting to burst through on the US Tour, is testament to his skills, and to that US 'production line.'

In recent years men like Scott Simpson, Bob Tway, Jeff Sluman and Larry Mize have become 'one hit wonders' and won a major before slipping into relative obscurity. But there have been others who have rolled off the 'production line' and made more of an impact on the world game.

Hal Sutton, Craig Stadler and Ben Crenshaw have been firm favorites with golfing fans both sides of the Atlantic, as has Payne Stewart, who eventually won his first major in 1989 when he captured the PGA title. But there are other men who, while they are still awaiting their first major triumph, have been typical of the American golf scene.

The tall upright Paul Azinger, the man with the unusual grip, has been the second biggest money winner to Curtis Strange in recent years. He is a confident, and talented player. His first major success must surely be not too far away. And what about Tom Kite? He is near the top of the all-time money list and has won ten Tour events but has never won a major. Surely he must be the best player never to have won one of golf's Big Four titles?

ABOVE: *Paul Azinger obviously enjoying the competition at the 1988 USPGA.*

RIGHT: *In 1989 Tom Watson overtook Jack Nicklaus as the biggest money winner but he has in turn lost that honour to Tom Kite. And he could soon be losing the top spot to Curtis Strange.*

And the host of US talent does not end there. Chip Beck has risen up the rankings rapidly in the last three seasons. Mark Calcavecchia won the British Open at Troon in 1989; but will he go the same way as Tway, Sluman, Mize and Simpson? Or will he continue to enjoy winning ways?

There are so many more names capable of becoming big money winners and top household names in the 1990s; Tom Byrum, Davis Love, Bob Lohr and Steve Pate have all won on the Tour and showed that they have the ability to be around for a long time. And a name to look out for in the 1990s could be that of Jay Don Blake. But even if those men do not make an impact there will always be plenty more talent ready to roll off the 'production line'. It has a habit of breeding top golfers and will be keen to confirm its ability to maintain the United States as the world's leading golf nation in the 1990s, just as it did in the 1960s, 70s and 80s.

BUT DON'T FORGET THE BRITISH

Britain too has produced a steady stream of quality golfers in the 80s as the sport continues to thrive following, firstly, the success of Tony Jacklin in winning the British and US Opens, and then Jacklin's victories as Ryder Cup captain.

In Nick Faldo, Sandy Lyle and Ian Woosnam, Britain proudly boasts three men who can rightly be described as world class and in winning the Masters in successive years, Lyle and Faldo have earned themselves a place among golf's elite. Ian Woosnam hasn't won a major, yet, but he is regarded as one of the world's finest golfers.

Nick Faldo turned professional in 1976 after a successful amateur career during which he won the British Youth's and English Amateur titles. He was in the Ryder Cup team at the age of 20 in 1977 and the following year he won his first Tour event when he captured the PGA

Championship. By 1981 he was one of the top money-winners on the European Tour but he wanted to try his skills on the American golf circuit. However, without achieving any success he returned to Britain in 1983.

At the end of that year he made one of the biggest, and most important decisions of his career; to change his swing. Despite winning over £140,000 and finishing top of the European money list in 1983 he still sought the advice of David Leadbetter and the pair of them set about designing a new swing for Faldo.

The following year Nick returned to the States and won the Sea Pines Heritage Classic to become the first Briton since Jacklin in 1972 to win in the United States. He then played a vital role in helping the European team to victory in the 1985 and 1987 Ryder Cups and in

LEFT: *Sandy Lyle had a memorable season in 1988 which included victory in the Masters, the first by a Briton. But sadly, his game fell away in 1989 and the season was a disaster by his high standards.*

RIGHT: *Nick Faldo, like Sandy Lyle, has won both the British Open and US Masters in the 1980s. Their performances have helped re-establish British golfers among the finest in the world.*

BELOW: *Faldo deep in concentration during the 1988 Open at Lytham. He could not retain the title which was won by Seve Ballesteros.*

the latter year he won the British Open at Muirfield when he played some of the most consistent golf ever seen by an Open champion. Faldo started a memorable 1989 by succeeding Sandy Lyle as Masters champion when he beat Scott Hoch at the second hole of the play-off. At the end of the year he was a member of the Ryder Cup team which retained the trophy at The Belfry.

Nick Faldo rebuilt his swing because he wanted a swing that would keep him at the top for many years. He is still young and has that all-important ingredient in his make-up, the desire to win. Combine the two and British golf has a champion in its midst for many years to come.

Sandy Lyle has also proved to be one of the greats of British golf in the 1980s. But sadly he had a setback in 1989 when he had a dis-astrous year which culminated in him asking to be left out of Tony Jacklin's Ryder Cup plans. But great golfers do not lie down for ever and Sandy should soon bring his immense power and talents back to the fore of world golf.

Curiously, although he represents Scotland at international level, Sandy was born in England, at Shrewsbury. Like Faldo he had a successful amateur career and represented England at the age of 14. Shortly after appearing in the 1977 Great Britain Walker Cup team he turned professional. He won his first professional event in 1978 when he captured the Nigerian Open, during which he shot a round of 61. A year later Sandy was top of the European money list . . . not bad for a professional of only two seasons.

He has since topped the money list on two more occasions, and in

ABOVE: *There is plenty of British talent in the wings. Howard Clark, for example, has been a professional since 1973 but in the second half of the 1980s has played some of the finest golf of his career which has been duly rewarded.*

ABOVE RIGHT: *Ronan Rafferty has successfully made the transition from top amateur at the start of the 1980s to top money winner on the European PGA Tour at the end of the decade.*

RIGHT: *Sandy Lyle must be regarded as one of the world's biggest hitters.*

1985 he ventured across the Atlantic to further his career. He returned to Britain a couple of months later to compete in the British Open at Royal St. George's and emerged as the first home winner since Tony Jacklin in 1969. On the US Tour Sandy had made a big impact with his long hitting, and he had become a favorite with the US fans. He had his first win on the Tour when he took the Greater Greensboro Open in 1986 and the following year he won the Tournament Players' Championship after a play-off against Jeff Sluman. But Sandy was saving his best for the 1988 season.

He won the Phoenix Open and Greater Greensboro Open, both after play-offs, against Fred Couples and Ken Green respectively. The week after his Greensboro success Sandy became the first British winner of the Masters. He took the lead on the second day and stayed at the head of the pack. But it was a magnificent 5-iron from a bunker on the last hole, to within 10 feet of the flag, that guaranteed Sandy a one stroke win over Mark Calcavecchia. It was one of Augusta's all-time great shots.

Ian Woosnam, unlike Faldo and Lyle, has not won a major, but he has certainly made his mark since turning professional in 1976 and has developed into one of the most powerful and feared golfers in the 1980s, both in Britain and the United States. Standing only 5ft 4½in tall, Woosnam generates awesome power and is one of the longest hitters in the world. Like Sandy Lyle, Woosnam was born in England but represents another country at international level; in his case, Wales.

The road to the top has been a long and hard one for Ian. He had to wait six years for his first Tour win, the 1982 Swiss Open, and since then he has been consistently among the top honors and has never been out of the top ten on the money list. His finest season was in 1987 when he was the top earner in Europe after winning five Tour events, including the World Match-Play title at Wentworth. In addition he helped Wales to win the World Cup and Woosnam took the individual prize to end a remarkable season in which he had also figured in the European team which won the Ryder Cup on US soil for the first time.

The winning has continued since that great year and in 1989 he came close to taking the US Open when he trailed the winner Curtis Strange by just one shot. In the US PGA championship he was in contention until eventually ending up three behind the champion Payne Stewart. But surely that first elusive major cannot be too far away for Ian Woosnam.

Britain is well endowed with talent to guarantee it a secure place in the world of golf in the 1990s. Woosnam, Faldo and Lyle will all be strong contenders for any title in the years to come, but there are also men like Mark James, Ronan Rafferty, Gordon Brand junior and Howard Clark who have all proved they can win against some of the best golfers in the world. It is not only the Americans who have a 'production line' capable of churning out golfing talent.

BELOW: *There was no stopping the diminutive Welshman Ian Woosnam in 1987. He won more than £1 million worldwide in the season and won the World Match-Play, team and individual World Cup titles, three European Tour events, plus many more.*

RYDER CUP '89 – THE GREAT HYPE

Since Tony Jacklin led the European team to a memorable Ryder Cup victory at The Belfry in 1985 the competition has enjoyed unprecedented interest. When he took his band of warriors to win the Cup on US soil for the first time in 1987 the media had a field day.

From the moment Jacklin and the trophy returned to Britain, plans were being made for the 1989 match, again to be held at The Belfry. Such was the interest that the 'hype' for Ryder Cup '89 started 18 months before the event. The three day tournament belongs to golf,

but in 1989 it also belonged to the marketing men and the free-flowing champagne in the hospitality tents. Ryder Cup '89 was to become not only a great sporting occasion, but also a great social occasion.

It was designated to be all-ticket, the first all-ticket golf match in Britain, and long before the first ball was struck every one of the 27,000 tickets for each day's play was sold out, and hotel rooms in the area were at a premium. The marketing men were delighted with their efforts. But at the end of the day the real winner was golf, as everybody who picked up a microphone at the closing ceremony kept reminding us.

After a magnificent first two days Tony Jacklin's men seemed to have the Cup well and truly won. But then it started falling apart in the singles. And the men who should have won; Ballesteros, Faldo and Langer, all lost. The responsibility placed on the other members of the European team was immense. How well men like Christy O'Connor and Jose-Maria Canizares coped, and it was Canizares, the oldest man in the match. who guaranteed the tie and thus retained the Ryder Cup for his side.

After his win over Ken Green there was an anti-climatic air about the rest of the proceedings. Tom Kite was quick to point out to a British television interviewer that Europe had *not* won the Cup, merely retained it. Raymond Floyd had to motivate his men into battling it out to the end and try and force a tie, which was secured when Curtis Strange beat Ian Woosnam. It was only the second tie in Ryder Cup history.

After all the tears, the hugging, the kissing, the interviews and the speeches, the Ryder Cup was locked away in a bank vault and the

ABOVE: *Gordon Brand junior (pictured) and his partner Sam Torrance gave Europe a badly needed win on the opening afternoon when they beat Strange and Azinger. Europe was trailing after the morning foursomes but came back to take the lead at the end of the first day.*

RIGHT: *Nick Faldo blasts one out of the bunker and into the hole. Luck like that can play a crucial role in match-play events like the Ryder Cup.*

LEFT: *Lanny Wakins is absolutely delighted at chipping in at the 18th on the opening day.*

LEFT: *Paul Azinger watches anxiously to see where his chip at the 17th has gone during his singles match with Seve Ballesteros.*

RIGHT: *Oh! the delight of it all. Jose Maria Canizares holes the putt which assures Europe of at least a draw and therefore retains the Cup.*

BELOW LEFT: *In his singles match Tom Kite beat Howard Clark 8 & 7. It is the biggest win since matches were first played over 18 holes in 1961.*

BELOW: *Nick Faldo expresses how he feels at missing a putt.*

thousands of fans made their way home, the golfers made their way to the next tournament and the marketing men made their way to the bank.

Ryder Cup '89 was about hype. But more importantly Ryder Cup '89 was about golf. It may all have been so different from the days of James Braid, Tom Morris and Harry Vardon, and the days of hickory-shafted clubs and feathery and gutty balls. But in the end the real winner *was* golf. The marketing aspect of the sport is here to stay. Golf has become a big money sport. But nobody can ever take away the wonderful spirit and competitive nature of this great game. Ryder Cup '89 showed us both aspects of the modern game.

Acknowledgments

The publisher would like to thank Ad Vantage who designed this book, Pat Coward who prepared the index and Mandy Little who researched the illustrations. The following agencies and individuals supplied the illustrations.

All-Sport: pages 2-3, 2(Insert Bottom), 4-5, 60, 61, 62(Both), 63, 117(Left), 121(Both), 124(Right & Top Left), 125 (Bottom Both), 128(Bottom), 130(Right), 136(Top Left & Bottom), 140(Top), 142-143, 144(All Three), 145, 146, 147, 148-149, 150-151(All Three), 152, 153, 155(All Three), 156(Top & Bottom Left), 158, 159(Both), 160-161(All Four), 162(Both), 163, 164(Top), 165(All Three), 166, 167(Bottom), 168(All Three), 169, 170, 171(Right), 172(Both), 173(Both).

ASSOCIATED PRESS: pages 65, 72(Bottom), 78-79, 81(Both), 84, 95(Bottom), 98, 102-103, 123(Both), 124(Left Bottom), 126(Bottom), 127(Top), 128(Top), 135(Bottom).

BETTMANN ARCHIVE: pages 118(Both), 127(Both Bottom), 131(Bottom), 133(Top), 136-137(Top), 138, 139(Top).

MICHAEL HOBBS GOLF COLLECTION/ALL-SPORT: pages 7, 8(Bottom), 11(Left), 13(Top), 15(Left), 16(Both), 17(Both), 19(Top), 20(Both), 21(Bottom), 24, 25, 26(Right Insert), 27(Top), 29(Bottom Left), 30, 31(Bottom), 36, 39(Bottom), 41(Both Bottom), 43(Top), 46(Right), 47(Both), 50(All Three), 51(Both), 52(Top), 53(Both), 67, 68(Bottom), 70(Both), 72(Top), 75(Both), 78(Both Left), 82(Left), 93, 95(Top), 99(Top), 101(Top Right), 103(Top), 106(Top), 111(Top Middle), 113(Right), 115(Bottom), 130(Left), 131(Top), 136(Right), 140(Bottom).

HULTON-DEUTSCH COLLECTION: pages 2(Insert Top & Middle), 22(Bottom), 34(Top), 39(Top), 41(Top), 46(Left), 64, 66, 73, 74, 76, 82(Right), 85, 86, 87(Bottom), 89(Bottom), 92, 94, 101(Bottom), 104-105, 108, 109, 110, 111(Bottom), 115(Top), 116(Left & Bottom), 117(Right), 119, 120(Bottom), 122, 125(Top), 129, 132-133, 133(Bottom), 134(All Three), 137(Bottom Left), 143.

MANSELL COLLECTION: pages 8(Top), 9(Bottom), 12(Left), 31(Both Top), 43(Bottom), 44-45.

THE MINNEAPOLIS INSTITUTE OF ARTS: page 9(Top).

BRIAN MORGAN GOLF PHOTOGRAPHY: pages 23(Top), 154, 157, 164(Bottom), 171(Left).

NATIONAL GALLERIES OF SCOTLAND/NATIONAL PORTRAIT GALLERY: pages 6, 10, 12(Right).

NATIONAL RAILWAY MUSEUM: page 29(Both Left).

PETER NEWARK'S PICTURES: page 13(Bottom).

WILLIAM S. PATON: pages 11(Both Right), 27(Bottom), 28, 29(Top & Middle), 22(Top), 23(Bottom), 54-55, 57, 58(Insert), 58-59, 137(Main Pic), 139(Bottom), 141, 156(Bottom Right), 167(Top).

ST. ANDREWS ROYAL & ANCIENT GOLF CLUB: pages 1, 37.

ST. ANDREWS UNIVERSITY, PHOTOGRAPH COLLECTION: pages 14, 15(Top Right & Bottom), 21(Top), 26(Top Two), 42, 48, 49, 52(Bottom).

THE SCOTSMAN PUBLICATION: pages 69(Bottom), 120(Top), 126(Middle).

SPORT & GENERAL: page 80.

US GOLF ASSOCIATION: pages 18, 19(Bottom), 32(Both) 33, 34(Bottom), 35, 38, 56, 68(Top), 69(Top), 71, 77(Both), 83, 87(Top), 88, 89(Both Top), 90(Both), 91, 96(Bottom), 97, 100, 106(Bottom), 107(Both), 113(Left), 114, 126(Top), 135(Top & Right).